Wicked
women
of the *Raj*

...unger is a dedicated Indophile having spent much of the ...years travelling and living in India. A native of Australia, ...ed a PhD in Indian History from the University of Sydney ...-authored a biography of Molly Fink, a woman from her ...who married the rajah of Pudukkottai in the early twentieth ...y. She also authored a controversial book on the Anglo-Indian ...unity.

...oralie has contributed many articles and papers on India to newspapers, magazines and academic forums and worked as a ...ant on an art exhibition, 'Dancing to the Flute', at the Art ...New South Wales.

...nt years she taught at the American International School, Chennai.

Coralie has six children, including triplets and twins, all of whom are ...w old India hands.

Wicked women of the Raj

EUROPEAN WOMEN WHO BROKE SOCIETY'S RULES
AND MARRIED INDIAN PRINCES

CORALIE YOUNGER

HarperCollins *Publishers* India
a joint venture with

INDIA TODAY GROUP

New Delhi

First published in India in 2003 by
HarperCollins *Publishers* India
a joint venture with
The India Today Group

Copyright © Coralie Younger 2003

Second impression 2003

Acknowledgements for photographs:
A.L. Syed; Annabella Parker; Nawab Iqbal Khan of Palanpur;
G.B. Singh of Jind; Younger Family Collection; H.M. Queen Elizabeth's Windsor
Castle Archives; Elsie Mudge.

HarperCollins *Publishers*
1A Hamilton House, Connaught Place, New Delhi 110 001, India
77-85 Fulham Palace Road, London W6 8JB, United Kingdom
Hazelton Lanes, 55 Avenue Road, Suite 2900, Toronto, Ontario M5R 3L2
and 1995 Markham Road, Scarborough, Ontario M1B 5M8, Canada
25 Ryde Road, Pymble, Sydney, NSW 2073, Australia
31 View Road, Glenfield, Auckland 10, New Zealand
10 East 53rd Street, New York NY 10022, USA

Typeset in 12/14 Adobe Garamond
Nikita Overseas Pvt. Ltd.

Printed and bound at
Thomson Press (India) Ltd.

To

Marina, Max, Toby, Keats, Connor, Alessandra

ACKNOWLEDGEMENTS

Thanks to the many contributors whose stories create the romance of *Wicked Women of the Raj*. Thanks to Gill Hewitt, who laboriously helped rework the text from its original form, and to Clare Forte, who designed the book and took such great pains with the pictures. Thanks to Judy Tenzing, who oversaw the final copy and made invaluable suggestions over steaming cups of Darjeeling tea and helped sustain my love of India through many conversations when the energy flagged.

Very special thanks to Sukhie Singh of Kapurthala, who gave much moral support when I fell ill at the end of my writing of this book. Thanks to Ed Duyker for his help with the chapter on Molly Fink.

Thanks to Renuka Chatterjee of HarperCollins India, who saw the great worth of these stories in this book when others did not and to Amit Agarwal for his patient and careful editing from across the world.

And thanks to my children, who were so much a part of the writing and research of this book, for their tolerance and support.

CONTENTS

FOREWORD   11

INTRODUCTION   15

THE PRINCES   39

BAMBA MULLER   43
*married Maharajah Duleep Singh of the Punjab, fifth
king of Lahore*

ADA DOUGLAS WETHERILL   43
married Maharajah Duleep Singh

FLORRIE BRYAN   58
married Maharajah Rajendar Singh of Patiala

OLIVE MONOLESCUE   67
married Ranbir Singh, maharajah of Jind

ANITA DELGADO   74
married Maharajah Jagatjit Singh of Kapurthala

EUGENIE GROSUPOVA   75
married Maharajah Jagatjit Singh of Kapurthala

DOLLY PARNELL   91
married Prince Nasir Ali Khan of Rampur

ELSIE THOMPSON   94
married Gopal Narain Singh, maharajah of Tikari

MOLLY FINK   115
   married Martanda Bhairava Tondaiman,
   rajah of Pudukkottai

MORAG MURRAY   138
   married Syed Abdullah of Koh Fort

NANCY MILLER   147
   married Maharajah Tukoji Rao Holkar of Indore

MOLLY ELSIP   160
   married Prince Ali Khan of Jaora

STELLA MUDGE   168
   married Paramjit Singh, maharajah of Kapurthala

MARGUERITE LAWLER   189
   married Yeshwant Rao Holkar, maharajah of Indore

EUPHEMIA CRANE   189
   married Yeshwant Rao Holkar, maharajah of Indore

JOAN FALKINER   201
   married Nawab Taley Mohamed Khan of Palanpur

SANDRA MCBRYDE   217
   married Hanwant Singh, maharajah of Jodhpur

YVONNE MARTIN   222
   married Nawabzada Mohamed Mubarak Abbasi
   of Bahawalpur

ANNABELLA PARKER   230
   married Bhagwat Singh, maharana of Udaipur

HELEN SIMMONS   243
   married Mukarram Jah Bahadur, nizam of Hyderabad

REFERENCES   255

FOREWORD

*A*fter spending three weeks on a camel caravan across the Great Thar Desert of Rajasthan, we finally reached Jaipur and were ensconced in an old maharajah's hunting lodge – camped in the grounds, I am sad to say, for, as Coralie and I often bemoaned (closet colonial memsahibs that we are!), we were born too late to be a part of the golden era of the British Raj in India. A century ago we might have been sipping nimbu panis on the verandah or preparing for a dinner-dance at the Officer's Club. Alas, those days were long gone but I was happy just to be in India, indulging the all-consuming passion for the subcontinent which Coralie and I have always shared.

As dusk approached my fellow caravaners and I were sitting by our tents sorting gear, emptying endless amounts of sand from bags, cameras and shoes when an old friend, Narpat Singh – a strikingly handsome fellow and junior member of the princely house of Bikaner in Rajasthan – asked if an Australian friend of his who was visiting Jaipur might join us for dinner at the lodge. Since our local camp staff always prepared enough food for a small regiment, we agreed.

The dinner invitation, it seemed, became a little hazy in its delivery and a little before dark Narpat arrived with his guest. The silence was deafening as this tall, willowy Australian woman dressed in an exquisite silk sari, her long golden hair perfectly braided, entered the compound. The look on her bespectacled face said it all – 'dinner at the Maharajah's Lodge' had come across rather differently from the reality of the event.

The woman was clearly most embarrassed and after an awkward few moments I walked over and was introduced by Narpat. 'This is Coralie Younger – from Sydney.' She graced our camp stools with her elegant presence and we talked for hours, forming the foundations of a bond and friendship which would last a lifetime.

Coralie was as obsessive about India as I was and it was delightful to find a kindred soul. She was researching her PhD on Australia's relations with India in the late nineteenth and early twentieth centuries and spent a great deal of time there to that end. However, one soon became acutely aware that most of Coralie's life energies and choices focused on India. While being a dutiful wife and mother, nothing could ever sway her in her resolve to learn more about India, spend more time there and immerse herself more completely in it. If ever there was a 'magnificent obsession', this was it. Even my devotion to the history and culture of this extraordinary nation paled before Coralie's knowledge and understanding of the subcontinent.

This is not to say, however, that her passion was blind, for she was aware of all the foibles, paradoxes and sheer frustrations that *are* India. In fact, in our more honest moments, we have both admitted to each other that we may in reality be ourselves anachronisms – 'memsahibs', romantics and dreamers hankering for a world, an era, a rich and extravagant culture which no longer exists. Such a world could not exist in our times and we accept that it is gone but how we loved to read and hear about it and what joy we always experienced in finding little pockets of that old grandeur – still rich and vibrant and alive. An exquisitely restored princely palace, the throne room of a medieval fortress, the silks and gems of the maharanis – or the many old-timers still alive who lived during those days and still recall and relive the grandeur.

Coralie's involvement with India throughout her adult life was deep and often painful – her experiences at once wonderful and tragic. It is this personal experience and the strength and determination with which she dealt with it all, which gives this book its life. In many ways she can be described as a 'wicked woman' of India – a memsahib bewitched and tantalized by the strange world around her. There is so much of Molly Fink in her character – and perhaps a little of Elsie Thompson as well. I doubt that another woman could have delved as deeply or understood more fully what drove these women in their lives in India. The character of the enquiring young woman in Ruth Prawer Jhabvala's novel *Heat and Dust* characterizes Coralie in so many ways – in her craving to be Olivia, mistress of the nawab, but still facing the harsh reality of living and making sense of the India of today.

Wicked Women of the Raj is an engaging and fascinating journey into a world all but gone. It presents an array of Western women from many parts of the world who lived extraordinary lives in extraordinary times. And in these rich and romantic tales you will find tantalizing glimpses and the insightful introspection of the author – that 'wicked woman', Coralie Younger.

Judy Tenzing
Sydney

INTRODUCTION

Except for the odd woman captured by pirates and sold into a Mughal harem, the first European woman to enter India owed her presence to the Portuguese. Following the route carved out by Portuguese officer Alfonso de Albuquerque in 1510, ships laden with unmarried Portuguese women set sail from Lisbon harbour, braved the pirate-infested sea lanes between Portugal and India, sailed up the sweetly languid waters of the Mandovi River to finally drop anchor at Old Goa, the capital of Portugal's Indian empire. There, the women, dressed in elegant mantilla and dainty lace, became the brides of lonely Portuguese officials languishing in their great empty rococo palaces with wrought iron balconies, slatted shutters of translucent oyster shells, terrazzo marble floors and ebonized rosewood furniture. The palaces were set amidst fields of tender rice paddy and sweeping coconut trees. The presence of king cobras and frogs in viscous pools made it clear that this indeed was the Tropics and not the Mediterranean.

Later, the East India Company followed the Portuguese example and it too brought out women from Britain in the expectation that they would marry and provide legitimate solace to lonely English merchants who had until then found relief in the arms of Indian women of lowly origins.

India's reputation as a rich marriage mart for European women continued right up until the demise of the British Raj in 1947. During India's cold weather season, women would sail out from England to India to plunder its plentiful store-house of bachelors regardless of the dangers of the tropical climate and a culture that bore no resemblance at all to the one they had known at home. These women came out with such regularity and with such transparent ambitions that they were unkindly dubbed the 'fishing fleet'. The failure to catch a husband was not viewed sympathetically, and women who returned to England unwed were rather brutally referred to as 'Returned Empties'. Their plight, depicted acerbically in a poem that appeared in the *Illustrated Weekly of India* in 1936, was unenviable.

> Now sail the chagrined fishing fleet
> Yo ho, my girls, yo ho!
> Back to Putney and by fleet
> Poor girls, you were too slow.

Women of the Raj esteemed as eminently marriageable possessed certain merits that might not necessarily have been those highly prized at home. Firstly it was expected that women who sought to marry into the Raj were not to be too clever or too well-educated. In British India, for females at least, intelligence was never thought to be a virtue. Secondly, an absence of sexual experience or even knowledge of the mechanics of intercourse, was taken as a given. On the other hand it was thought proper to sublimate excess energies (especially sexual) on exercise, and so a proficiency at sports came to be valued, with riding, tennis, golf and shooting preferred. Hobbies like sewing, flower arranging, music and sketching were not only thought desirable but were deemed utilitarian as well as socially acceptable. Such skills and the ability to run a smart household were highly prized as the colonial lifestyle required continual moves, often into rural localities and other barren terrain where household furnishings and foodstuffs were not always readily accessible or, if they were available, were extremely expensive. Women in India learned to make do.

A shared or not dissimilar social background was also considered a prudent marriage consideration. If a man and a woman belonging to different backgrounds ignored convention and insisted on marriage, it was thought unusual enough to draw considerable comment and invariably some censure and derision. In *Women of the Raj*, Margaret McMillan tells the tale of a young governess travelling out to India, her status as a teacher of children to be the lowest of the low in an English household. She has the good fortune whilst on board ship to become engaged to a member of the Indian Civil Service. McMillan writes that the way in which the girl was commended by a fellow passenger for having 'caught' herself one of the 'heaven born', as the ICS were popularly known, confirms that the prevailing opinion was that a girl of her class must have employed some artifice to catch a man of such superior social standing.

Courtship between men and women of the Raj was carried out in a fashion similar to home in Britain but was done in an almost hothouse environment. Dances, suppers, sports, amateur theatricals, balls, parties and picnics; all, of course, suitably supervised by older married women, were the occasions at which men and women might meet and pledge their troth. At dances and suppers, the need for privacy was recognized by the furnishing of secluded spots with sofas surrounded by massed flowers and ferns where couples were able to sit out dances in solitude and thereby further romantic aspirations.

When a couple finally made the decision to marry, there was an attempt to celebrate the occasion as much like home as possible. Wedding photographs of European couples in India possess all the trappings of their counterparts in Britain and Europe: the long white dress and veil, the flowers, the bouquet, the attendants, the men in formal suits or dress uniforms, the wedding cake and wedding guests all looking as though they are situated in Surrey or Cirencester except at the edges, where a brown-skinned bearer or the Indian landscape intrudes.

Honeymoons were invariably brief and, if time permitted, were spent in one or other of the numerous hill stations that the British had created for themselves in more salubrious climes all over India. After snatching a few days of relaxation, it was back to shouldering the White Man's Burden and fitting into the role that was strictly laid down according to one's rank in the machinery of the Raj. As married life took hold, the qualities a husband sought were those of an affectionate wife and, in time, a tender mother.

The memoirs, diaries, letters and travelogues of women who went out to India give the impression that they served a subsidiary function as mere appendages of the male members of the British Raj. But the stories of wives and daughters of the Raj are only a part of the picture. There were teachers like Annette Ackroyd and Florence Wyld, a clergyman's daughter who became principal of Hyderabad's Mahbubia school for high-caste girls. There were governesses like Norma Shastri, who left Chicago to take up employment with the maharajah of Gwalior and ended up marrying a Hindu brahmin and settling permanently in Madras. There was Gladys Stewart, who went out to teach the family of the deputy commissioner of Garhwal and whose first adventure on arriving in India, learning how to mount and hang on to Lakshmi, the commissioner's official elephant, was only the first of many adventures she was to experience in the country. There were women like Muriel Le Mesurier, who acted as escort to the three older daughters of Sir Roger Lumley, the governor of Bombay, and who later said of her vocation, 'I didn't really want to teach, but I did want to travel.'

India invigorated the artistic impulse of writers Constance Sitwell, Ethel Anderson, Maud Diver, Ethel Savi, Isobel Savory and Josephine Ransom. It enriched the writing of journalist Emma Roberts and brightened the canvases of painter Florence Fuller, who expressed her artistic impulses in the serene surroundings of Madras' Theosophical Society.

Travellers Fanny Parks, Emily Eden, Margaret Harkness, Fanny Maria Monk and Australia's Ethel Kelly recorded their experiences in vivid prose for incredulous readers back home. Many women travelled under the aegis of British approval and security. Ruby Madden, daughter of Sir John Madden, Victoria's lieutenant-governor and chief justice, journeyed to India to attend the imperial durbar of 1903 and sketched her impressions.

There were women who worked in India during the First and Second World Wars as nurses in British hospitals: nurses like Anne Donnell who recorded her vivid impressions in *Letters of an Australian Army Sister* and the five hundred Australian nurses who were sent to India in 1915 to release British nurses for duty at the front.

Sister Narelle Hobbes, who served with Queen Alexandra's Imperial Military Nursing Service Reserve and was invalided to India from Mesopotamia in 1917, wrote of the plains of Central India, '... absurdly like Australia, first it was just like Bre country in a very good season, then it got sort of red hilly country like Cobar ...'

As Hobbes' health deteriorated despite convalescence up in the cooler climes of Almora in the Indian Himalayas, her spirits were temporarily lifted by its 'mountains like nothing in Australia'. In the depths of despair at an illness that gradually gnawed away at her energy, Hobbes' mind soared and found physical and spiritual solace in the Himalayas; so much so that she wanted her family to share in their ethereal beauty,

... how I wish you could see it all, how you would
love it, at times it is almost overpowering in its
beauty, there is too much of it, so it seems, but it
is a thing to dream of, and I sometimes wonder what
I have ever done, to deserve all this pleasure ...

It was India that sustained Hobbes' spirit and kept alive a
body that only succumbed when she finally took the ship back
to Australia.

The needs of the spirit were what drew another distinct
group of women to India, a group that in terms of size was
second only to the wives and daughters of the men who served
the Raj. These were the missionaries: women who went out
to India to save the 'benighted Hindoo' and to save Indian
women 'imprisoned' in the harem or the zenana. The zenana
missions for women and American Amy Carmichael's mission, Dohnavur, in south India, established for abandoned
babies and child prostitutes, were Christian groups run by
women for women.

Women missionaries who went out to India were mostly
drawn from middle-class homes, often with a history of service
to the community. From where they stood, India's women
seemed degraded and downtrodden. The missionaries sought
the upliftment of Indian women from what they believed to
be the evils of child marriage, child widowhood, female
infanticide, polygamy and purdah.

It was the sequestered space of the zenana that served as
a metaphor for missionaries and others back home of all that
was evil in India. In Reverend T.B. Fischer's *A Month in India*,
zenana missionary Isabelle Bishop described:

I have lived in zenanas and harems, and have seen
the daily life of the secluded women, and I can

speak from bitter experience of what their lives are – the intellect dwarfed, so that the woman of twenty or thirty years of age is more like a child of eight intellectually, while all the worst passions of human nature are stimulated and developed in a fearful degree.

The zenana was believed to pose such risks that it was thought Indian women were not alone in being compromised by life inside its walls. An anonymous 'district judge' wrote a letter to the *Friend of India*, warning the churches against sending young unmarried European ladies to the houses of 'Hindoos' claiming,

> ... that the system of family life among the secluded females of a hindoo household is quite inconsistent with the idea of any protection from familiarity or insult from the male members of the household being afforded by the ladies of the zenana.

Whilst the 'district judge' insisted on the delicacy of missionary women, they proved otherwise, shouldering a variety of strenuous burdens while often leaving the proselytisation to their male counterparts. For women, preaching the word of God was translated into a matter of action speaking louder than words. They were supremely practical women. They were not afraid to get their hands soiled or take enormous risks. Many taught, others set up dispensaries and carried out minor surgical procedures, others nursed the sick and dying, many taught preventive health according to Western ideals of hygiene. Doctors Ida Scudder and Christian Rogan, who worked in Vellore and Dohnavur respectively, shouldered medical responsibilities they would never have contemplated back home in

America and Scotland. India allowed them the freedom to explore the limits of their professional capabilities which would have been impossible in the conventional confines of the patriarchal societies from where they came.

While most European women who ventured out to India conformed to some sort of conventional structure, there were opportunities here for women to lose themselves, invent themselves or to find themselves as Ida Scudder and Christian Rogan proved. Scudder and Rogan, like other women, used India as a catalyst to find themselves and their life's mission.

A group of European women who used India in a less conventional, spiritual sense were the female members of the Theosophical Society, most notably its president Annie Besant. The original founders of Theosophy, Helen Blavatsky and Colonel Olcott, had been drawn to India by the primacy that it afforded spiritual and philosophical questions. Land in the southern suburbs of Madras was turned into the society's headquarters and attracted female as well as male acolytes to its park-like grounds sweeping down to the Bay of Bengal and the Adyar river.

Theosophy's most famous follower, Annie Besant, allied herself with India's Home Rule movement, becoming a friend and confidante of its leading nationalists. She was a brilliant orator who gave stirring diatribes against Britain's imperium. She was not afraid to speak out publicly against Britain for plundering India's material wealth, cautioning it to look to the spiritual treasures that India had to offer, to take those gratefully and, in turn, give India her freedom.

While Theosophists were viewed by official British Indian society as somewhat unorthodox and, at times, even politically dangerous, there were other women who acted even more like unbecoming daughters of the Empire. Women like Margaret Noble, who, after meeting Swami Vivekananda, converted to

Hinduism and assumed the Indian name of Sister Nivedita. Women like poet Adela Cory, who married Colonel Malcolm Nicolson and cross-dressed as a Pathan in order to follow him to the dangerous frontier territory between India and Afghanistan. Cory published the exotically themed *The Garden of Kama* in 1902 but, distraught upon her husband's premature death in 1904, killed herself before she could reap the rewards of her poems' success.

Ursula Graham Bower, a patriot if not wholly conventional, was popularly dubbed the Naga Queen. She took up the Sten gun and rallied a group of Naga commandos around her during the Second World War to fend off the invading Japanese forces threatening India's northeast frontier. Similarly militarily inclined was James Hall, the Spanish-born wife of a Madras barrister who assumed Mughal-style dress and commanded a battalion of women guarding the nizam of Hyderabad's harem.

Madeleine Slade was an Englishwoman who possessed impeccable social antecedents. Her father was an admiral and she was raised in a genteel environment. Yet her decision to join Mahatma Gandhi and serve him devotedly as Miraben until Nathuram Godse's bullet felled him in the garden of Birla House, was viewed by many of her contemporaries as eccentric and decidedly un-British. Slade's encounter with Gandhi and India changed her completely. India provided the perfect milieu within which Slade and others could reinvent themselves.

Whilst the Besants and Slades and Bowers were viewed by official India as unconventional, they were nonetheless still not the type of women whom Britain saw as posing the greatest threat to European prestige and power. To this group belonged women of India's European underclass: the bar-maids (India's viceroy Lord Curzon especially targeted these as lowering the prestige of the ruling race), circus performers and the like; women who got drunk in public and became the paramours of low class European men who were working in cigar shops, as con men, variety performers, mercenaries, pimps and bar owners.

Women who had sexual relations with Indians did so for a variety of reasons. There were women whose occupation it was to service men for a fee, whether they were black or white or orange! There were European women who had extramarital affairs with Indians and there were women who married Indians either for love or money or position.

Most abhorrent to the Christian churches operating in India were members of India's European underclass, the white women who inhabited the cities' brothels.

European prostitutes in India were concentrated in the two great metropolises of Bombay and Calcutta. Many of the women had come to India simply to continue the profession they had been employed in at home in Britain and Europe. Many were alleged to be (perhaps more kindly than truthfully) the victims of the 'white slave' trade that was believed to be rampant between Europe and India. Others slipped into the occupation by default: in *Prostitution in Nineteenth and Early Twentieth Century Calcutta*, B. Joardar writes that female employees of the many opera companies, circuses and variety companies touring India often found themelves left high and dry when the companies went broke and the women were then forced into the trade by economic necessity. Others went into prostitution because the pay scales under which they worked as conjurors, dancers and actresses were so low that they looked to selling their bodies as a way to supplement meagre earnings.

Whatever the impetus, European prostitutes were operating in India from the earliest days, beginning with the East India Company shipping out unmarried women as brides for its officers. Women who failed to secure husbands or did not find a partner to their liking, lapsed into what the company denounced as a deterioration of morals. The council of the East India Company, in a minute to the deputy governor, noted:

> Whereas some of these women are grown scandal-ous to our nation, religion and government interest, we require you to give them fair warning that they do apply themselves to a more sober and Christian conversation.

When the women continued to ignore the government's warning, it was decided 'the sentence is that they shall be confined totally of their liberty to go abroad and fed with bread and water'. However, the company had to own some responsibility for the women's actions for bringing out to India in the first place what they termed 'gentlewomen' and 'other women'.

The Christian churches in Bombay and Calcutta were quick to denounce European prostitutes who were setting such a bad example to the 'natives'. White women selling their bodies to European men was bad enough but the idea of them serving Indians and men of mixed race was totally repugnant to these churches.

In Bombay, European prostitutes were concentrated at Cursetji Sukhlaji Street in the Kamathipura area. Here, the missionaries who formed themselves into a vigilante midnight mission to stamp out the nefarious practice found themselves, whilst patrolling the street, showered with water and oil and other unpleasant fluids by prostitutes occupying the upper floors of the street's buildings. In response, the midnight missionaries changed their attack and decided to man each end of the thoroughfare in order to harass the men who attempted to enter and patronize Cursetji Street's brothels. The missionaries complained that the verbal abuse and discomfort of drenching fluids and the assault by enraged clients was nothing compared to women missionaries' having to suffer the indignity of being mistaken for the 'unfortunates'.

Equally distressing was the fact that many of the prostitutes did not consider themselves ill used at all and did not want to be rescued. Fanny Epstein and Annie Gould had run away from England to set up a 'saloon bar' in Bombay's Kamathipura area. But they became the subject of official intervention after complaints from their parents and unsuccessful attempts to rescue them. The girls told the authorities they didn't want rescuing and had come to Bombay and their occupation of their own free will. Similarly, in 1894, the Russian ambasssador approached Prime Minister Gladstone's foreign secretary for help in finding and repatriating one Dina Gontcharoff who, he said, was being exploited in a maison de tolerance in India. She was finally located in Jinny Kraft's brothel in Kamathipura where she told investigators she was working of her own volition. As Gontcharoff had already been employed as a prostitute in Odessa before she came to India, the foreign office told the Russian ambassador they were powerless to intervene.

Though claims of a flourishing 'white slave trade' were probably exaggerated, there were a number of European men in Bombay and Calcutta who did serve as procurers of, and traffickers in, European women. Economic hardship and prevailing political expediencies that led to Jewish refugees fleeing persecution in eastern Europe, saw many of the women enter India where they took up prostitution as a means of survival.

The *Sentinel*, which prided itself as being the leading Protestant paper of western India, saw European prostitution as more visibly repugnant than its Indian counterpart. The *Sentinel* agonized over the fact that in Kamathipura, European women could be seen in the middle of the roadway wearing only a loose nightdress, unfastened, and worn with a pair of slippers. It decried the example such women set for the Indian population:

> No educated Native thinks he has properly 'done' Bombay unless he has seen the seething hell of European vice. The Native streets of vice are decorous in the extreme compared with Cursetji Sukhlaji Street. The women are decently clothed and many of them veiled, and the contrast is most humiliating.

Calcutta, Bishop Thoburn complained, was no better. He called its European prostitutes 'moral lepers' who took possession of houses that should have been occupied by decent people and thereby depressed the value of real estate. Miss E. Maxey, the superintendent of Calcutta's Diocesan Home, complained of brothel owner Marie Rosenthal operating premises in Calcutta's Wellington Street. Likewise Reverend Father W.H. Hart complained about Maggie Reid, who ran a brothel in Free School Street, while Reverend Father Naish objected to Natalia Zerska using Free School Street as a brothel under the guise of a cigar shop.

In 1894, pressure upon Calcutta's police commissioner by the city's Social Purity Group saw the inhabitants of four brothels on Elliot Road leave India entirely and those of three others move to different parts of Calcutta. But community pressure against prostitution in one city inevitably saw a concomitant outflow of prostitutes into one or the other of the big cities. It never really succeeded as a complete deterrent.

Missionary presssure on the authorities had mixed results. Police officials would, given the opportunity, have preferred to leave the women alone. The women naturally resented harassment·explaining that they were only plying their trade and minding their own business. In 1893, Sara Kameoski and twenty-seven other residents of Bombay's Cursetji Street called for protection from the police against the midnight missionaries, describing themselves as 'defenceless European women'. Moreover, not surprisingly, the customers, among them many prominent men, wanted the practice left well alone. They resented the interference of midnight missionaries like Malcolm Moss who obtained a tricycle,

> ... and follows home the carriages of some of the aristocratic official frequenters of the great European vice market of Bombay, finds their names and addresses, then sends them through the post letter of religious advice, tracts and purity literature.

Whilst prostitution took hold, extramarital relations as a practice were not scorned by a society that saw its women take flight every hot season into the cooler climes of the morally relaxed hill stations. In Simla, Mussoorie and Ooty it was taken for granted that married women and men on leave were free to indulge their passions as long as they were relatively discreet. For example, at the lavish balls, dinner parties and receptions held at the maharajah of Kapurthala's residence in Mussoorie, the best wines and champagne flowed freely while tables groaned with fine French food prepared by Parisian chefs. The maharajah's military secretary wrote that evenings concluded with men and women taking advantage of the privacy afforded by the Chateau de Kapurthala's large and densely planted gardens.

Yet affairs between European women and Indian men were always exceptional and considered beyond the pale. Evidence of prevailing attitudes appears in the *Englishman* which carried a report of a divorce case between a member of the Bengal Police and his errant wife. The cuckolded husband complained to the judge not so much about his wife's infidelity as about the partner with whom his wife had erred: 'I remonstrated with her for being so low as to misconduct herself with a native.'

Missionary Mary Pigot, in charge of Calcutta's Church of Scotland zenana mission and orphanage, found herself at the centre of controversy when accused, amongst other misdemeanours, of enjoying overly intimate contact with an Indian Christian. Eventually Pigot was cleared of misconduct but the public interest the case evoked was in large part a response to the European-Indian nexus. In similar fashion, Louis Bromfield's novel *The Rains Came* reflects the prevailing attitudes to mixed-race relations, with its aristocratic Lady Heston accepting that she could never attain happiness with her Indian doctor prince no matter how altruistic and decent he was. She ultimately chooses death as preferable to an ignominious life with her Indian beloved. Similarly, in *Heat and Dust*, Ruth Prawer Jhabvala constructs an unsettling end for her English girl diarist and her lover Inder Lal despite their love affair being enacted in the more racially liberal atmosphere of post-Independence India.

But the persistence of mixed-race liaisons, often cultivated by European women as much as by Indian men, reveals the speciousness of arguments that located lascivious aspirations and desire for physical union solely with the Indian male. Evidence of official recognition that the desire for mixed race unions often resided with European women was demonstrated in Viceroy Lord Curzon's expressed fear to adhere to the king's request to invite Indian orderlies to attend his court. He feared the attraction Indian men held for European women.

The woman aspect of the question is rather a difficulty, since strange as it may seem English women of the housemaid class, and even higher, do offer themselves to these Indian soldiers, attracted by their uniform, enamoured of their physique, and with a sort of idea that the warrior is also an Oriental prince.

Similarly, at Australia's Federation in 1901, a front cover of the *Bulletin* newspaper encapsulated the fears of a nation in its depiction of an Indian soldier tickling the chins of two well-dressed white women who look on adoringly, inclining their bodies provocatively towards their soldier prince. In other issues, the *Bulletin* regretted the practice of Englishwomen running after Indian men in the hope that all were Indian princes.

The problem of relations between Indian princes and white women was taken up by literature. Writers of fiction expressed the reality of relations between the princes and white women, at the same time perpetuating the myth that the impetus for union lay with the Indian male whether prince or commoner. Ruth Prawer Jhabvala's *Heat and Dust* proves the exception in that her nawab and Olivia appear equally to desire physical union although it is the nawab who makes the first overtures towards Olivia. On a different level, in *The Anglo-Indians*, Alice Perrin writes of the love of a young Indian prince for the heroine Fay Fleetwood. In keeping with prevailing attitudes the hero of Perrin's novel, Clive Somerton, felt,

... that primitive sense of repulsion innate in white-skinned humanity towards the notion of race admixture with a dark-skinned people – a repulsion arising from Nature's tendency to breed upwards, not downwards.

Similarly, in William Archer's play, *The Green Goddess*, the central character is an Indian prince who abducts an English girl in what is a theme conforming to prevailing stereotypes of the lascivious Indian male lusting after the white woman. The Indian male, invariably a prince, can only win the beautiful white woman by force. Naturally, at the end of Archer's play, RAF bombers appear over the zenana to rescue the white heroine from ravishment.

Mindful of the possibilities of princely encounters with white women, the government did its best to discourage the visits to Britain and the continent of what Viceroy Curzon called princely flaneurs and pleasure seekers. However, though the government might curtail the princes' visits to Europe, they could not stop them altogether, for the princes soon learned that illness, properly authenticated with doctor's certificates, provided the opportunity to take the cure in the popular spas and health resorts of Europe and Britain.

Once liaisons did take place, the government was at a loss as to how to deal with them. In *Princely India*, Clark Worswick refers to the princes' women as 'a dizzying array of manicurists, schoolgirls, nightclub entertainers, and American women of "doubtful antecedents".' The wife of an English jockey, caught in flagrante delicto in a Paris hotel with Maharajah Hari Singh of Kashmir, was the most notorious of the European women who encouraged these wealthy but gullible potentates. The Hari Singh incident, which came to be known as the 'Mr A' case, was dragged through the courts and splashed across the newspapers of Europe and America. The press revealed how the maharajah had been deliberately set up by his ADC Captain Arthur in order to extort money and blackmail him to the tune of £125,000.

Whilst the princes cavorted amidst the clubs and salons of Europe with a growing array of unsuitable European women,

India proved no better. Here too it seemed women were more than willing to consort with the princes even though the government might sneer at the social antecedents of some of the women. Moreover, women residing in Britain and Europe were more than happy to accept the princes' offers of an all-expenses-paid trip out to India where they could live in the lap of luxury.

In 1896, the Gaekwar of Baroda was cited in official correspondence for seducing a well-connected European woman, which resulted in the birth of a child. The Gaekwar then took jewels from the state treasury to bestow on his mistress, which further alienated his Indian wife. As a result, in a public gesture of rebuke, the maharani refused to meet his ship in Bombay upon his return from Europe. Even worse, given the Indian context, the maharani refused to send the children to greet their father, a gesture which resulted in violent scenes. But even so, the Gaekwar was far from chastened.

The fact that his maharani was the president of the 'All India Women's Conference', concerned with women's rights and education, may have emboldened her to write an open letter to the *Bombay Chronicle* bemoaning the treatment of princes' wives, likening them to mere chattel. Notwithstanding the maharani's outburst, in 1925 the government received a request from the Gaekwar's Hungarian mistress, whom he'd met in Paris, asking for a visa to spend three or four months in Baroda. The government said it had no objection to the request so long as no scandals ensued.

In 1903, the rajah of Pudukkottai had enraged official society by having an affair with a Mrs Reid, the wife of a Major Reid who was stationed in Bombay. Major Reid was an unsavoury character who had a reputation for running up unpaid gambling debts. It was these debts that the authorities believed led Major Reid to 'encourage' his wife to take up with the rajah for financial considerations.

The rajah lodged Mrs Reid in his guest house Nutshell, in Kodaikanal, spending most of his time with her there and ignoring his princely duties in Pudukkottai. Mrs Reid was said to be quiet and ladylike, the mother of a daughter of ten years who was understandably upset by the talk of her mother and the rajah and she reputedly asked at the club in Kodaikanal why the British members would not 'know' her mother.

The British were desperate to put an end to the affair, calling upon the military authorities to force Mrs Reid to return to her husband. The army responded saying they had no jurisdiction over Mrs Reid and therefore could not intervene in the matter. The authorities then decided to put pressure on the rajah by threatening that the prince of Wales would not receive him at Madras on his forthcoming visit to India in January 1906.

The British were encouraged to end the liaison by the fact that the Indians were as incensed as they were by the rajah's conduct. The Indian community implored the British to help put an end to what they thought was 'a disgraceful affair'.

Eventually the relationship died abruptly and Mrs Reid departed, reportedly satisfied with the expensive jewellery and cheques of considerable value that the rajah had bestowed upon her. Afterwards, the rajah's cottage, Nutshell, came to be known in official correspondence as the 'Love Cottage' and the whole affair as the Love Cottage incident.

But, to Britain's despair, Mrs Reid was to be only one of a number of European women with whom the rajah consorted. He later caused considerable chagrin by becoming engaged to an American woman.

Similarly, women found the good humoured and generous Maharajah Gopal Narain Singh of Tikari extremely appealing.

Bertine Kempster, the wife of the commandant of his Gurkha bodyguard, was merely one of a long line of European women with whom Rajie (as he was affectionately known) had relations, culminating in his marriage to an Australian actress he met and married in India in 1908.

French women were preferred by the avowedly Francophile Maharajah Jagatjit Singh of Kapurthala, whom author Rosita Forbes called a ruler 'whose spiritual home might well be Versailles'. In 1924 the maharajah paid all expenses for Madamoiselle Seret to sail out to India and companion him. Seret was lodged in the palace in Kapurthala, a town described by Forbes as 'a scrap of Paris laid at the foot of the Himalayas'.

The maharajah had been complaining to officials for some time that Indian women neither satisfied nor interested him and that the few months he spent in India each year were a penance unless he was accompanied by his European mistress. He threatened that if he could not bring Seret out to India then he would marry a European or stay away from his state for much longer than the six months of the year he was already absent. Initially, the government had been concerned that Seret might embarrass them by appearing as the maharajah's hostess at functions attended by European officials. But eventually, the government gave in to the maharajah's demands, persuaded that they could depend on the maharajah to be discreet.

In 1925, Madamoiselle Seret was followed by Madamoiselle Henriette Serrurier. Serrurier's maid told authorities her mistress had journeyed out to India specifically with the intention 'to make her fortune' by joining an Indian prince. On arrival in Bombay, Serrurier was met by a Mrs Barron and Captain Barron, the captain an unsavoury character who had seen service in many regiments throughout India. At the time of Serrurier's visit, he was in charge of the Kapurthala state stables.

Immigration officials were suspicious of the Barrons and Madamoiselle Serrurier, reporting to authorities that Mrs Barron was confused about where she and the captain stayed in India though eventually she answered with some hesitation that they lived in Lahore on the Mall. Mrs Barron answered queries about her husband, saying that he had served in so many regiments that she could not remember their names. But despite reservations, customs finally cleared the dubious trio and Serrurier was escorted by the Barrons to the Taj Mahal Hotel where she was registered under the maharajah's name.

Only six weeks after Madamoiselle Serrurier's arrival, Madame Lemma L. Izzat Pasha, who was described as fair, English-speaking and attired in European dress, arrived in Bombay and was received at the docks by the maharajah's military secretary Jarmani Dass. As Serrurier was, Pasha was escorted to the Taj Mahal Hotel and she too was registered under the maharajah's name. One can only marvel at the maharajah's audacity in inviting both women to stay as his guests at the same hotel within weeks of each other. But the staff at Bombay's Taj Mahal Hotel had become well accustomed to the princes' lothario-like behaviour in what was for the princes a home away from home.

Diwan Jarmani Dass was like the Taj staff, quite au fait in dealing with the arrangements required for the care and comfort of his master's European mistresses. In *Maharani*, Dass records his observations of the relationships the princes enjoyed with their European and Indian women. He noted how Jagatjit Singh was particularly performance-oriented in his relations with white women and as a Sikh would pray over the Granth Sahib, Sikhdom's holy book, for strength and vigour before spending the night with his mistress. In an expansive mood after a particularly successful evening spent with Seret, Jagatjit bestowed on her a jewelled collar by Cartier. Leaving her apartments, Jagatjit then proceeded to express his good humour by bestowing silver rupees on his patient courtiers who had been waiting outside for him to complete his lovemaking.

European barmaids serving Indian clients, drunken and disorderly white women, European women selling their bodies to Indian men, white women having extramarital relations with Indians, all of these were behaviours that threatened the prestige and so the very racial foundations of the empire upon which the superiority of the white race was based. But more than any of these, the fact of European women actually marrying Indian men, thereby acknowledging a physical and emotional equality, threatened psychologically to destabilize the Raj's racial and class hierarchy.

In a sense, the Raj's racial and class hierarchy merely reflected India's own caste hierarchy in that everyone knew their place and abided by it. Things worked when people knew the rules of the game and played by them. High-class princes marrying low-class European women, black men marrying white women, posed disharmonies. Failure to play by the rules, an ethos so beloved of the British in India, threatened chaos and the break-down of society. Whilst marriages between low-class white women and ordinary Indian men were abhorrent to the Raj, these unions could be ignored more effectively than the marriages of European women to the high-profile princes. Such marriages evoked a whole range of punishments and opprobriums that were felt keenly by some women and ignored by others.

Who were these women who went against all the conventions of their day and what were they like? Were they gold-diggers or were they hopeless romantics, hoping to re-enact their own Cinderella fairytale with a handsome prince? Did they live happily ever after?

Were these women no different from other women who ventured out to the subcontinent hoping to use it as a place where new identities could be worked out and forged? Or were these women looking to marriage with an Indian prince to transform them from low-class opportunists to princesses at the very pinnacle of society? Perhaps they were merely hoping to make a place for themselves in the sun?

Whatever their motives, one thing is certain. For these women – rich or poor, romantic or realist – India was the unknown of Milton's 'gorgeous east, ... showering on her kings barbaric pearl and gold'.

The Chamber of Princes in the late 1920s

THE PRINCES

*I*f India was the jewel in Britain's imperial diadem, then the Indian princes were the facets of that gem which glittered with an almost blinding incandescence. Rudyard Kipling wrote how 'providence created the Maharajahs to offer mankind a spectacle', the like of which will never be seen again.

As an institution, rajahs were as old as the Mahabharata and most probably dated from even earlier – from the Aryans. The Hindu notion of kingship always involved reciprocity: between the rajah, the king, and the praja, his people. The rajah was expected to protect his people from harm while they, in turn, paid him tribute in the form of agricultural produce, belongings and often their women.

Rajahs survived the Mughal invasion and its setting up of an imperial locus in Delhi. Moreover, as the power of the Mughal emperors waned, their offshoots, sometimes soldiers of fortune, sometimes successful dacoits, as well as their Hindu adversaries, seized more and more power and consolidated their position. Hindu kings were joined by Muslim nawabs, nizams and mirs, Hindu maharajahs, or great kings, and, in the case of Bhopal, begums (female rulers).

Indian kings could boast the singular achievement of not one of their assembly having ever been assassinated by their subjects, no matter how oppressive and cruel the ruler's regime.

In 1858, when the British Crown assumed formal rule of India in the wake of the 1857 Mutiny, the British confirmed the rajahs in their ascendancy, but now these kings owed obedience to the crown, in place of the Delhi emperor. They had to bend the knee to the British monarch and her representative in India, the viceroy.

This period saw a shift from kingship to princedom. The British discouraged the term 'king' in reference to Indian rulers. That was the prerogative of the British monarch. They instituted a means of control over the rajahs which involved the award of medals and decorations, and most important of all – gun salutes. If a ruler successfully ingratiated himself with the British, then he might see his gun salute raised; if he displeased, it was reduced. By such means Indian kings, like it or not, became puppets in the imperial drama.

From 1857 to 1947, three-fifths of the subcontinent was governed directly as British India. The remaining two-fifths, comprising six hundred thousand square miles, was the realm of the rajahs. Here, as long as they played by imperial rules, the princes could rule as they had of old. For following the 1857 Mutiny, the British were loath to interfere in matters of Indian religion and culture. The princes therefore had carte blanche to indulge every whim and fancy so long as it devolved on entertainment and pleasure, and did not upset the canons of the British Empire. One of the most sacrosanct of these was that there was to be no interracial marriage.

Viceroy Lord Curzon, who was the British monarch's representative in India at the turn of the twentieth century when India truly was the jewel in the imperial crown, was one of the princes' greatest admirers. He thought they embodied the noblest ideals of chivalry, good manners and honour, and warned that should the institution ever disappear, 'Indian society will go to pieces like a dismasted vessel in a storm'.

The rajahs' and maharajas' lifestyles were the stuff of make-believe: Aladdin's Cave and King Solomon's Mines rolled into one. Peter Pan's magic could never have conjured up such a world; a world that today even the princes look back upon in wonder. The maharajah of Indore could sink his arms up to the elbows in his treasure chests of diamonds; he was the possessor of peerless diamond earrings of 46 and 44 carats each. The maharajah of Baroda owned a seven-string pearl necklace estimated in 1903 to be worth seven million dollars. The nizam of Hyderabad owned the 227-carat Nizam diamond and the Jacob diamond of 174 carats, plus a gold coin called the Jahangir Nazarana that weighed eleven kilograms. The legendary Baroda Royal Pearl carpet offered for sale in Geneva in 1989 was conservatively valued at thirty-one million dollars.

The princes kept Rolls Royce in business. It custom-designed the car in every conceivable shape, material and colour. There were gold- and silver-plated models upholstered in the finest silk brocades and woven with pure gold and silver zari.

When Maharajah Jagatjit Singh of Kapurthala invited his French girlfriend Germain Pelligreno out to India for the cold season, he chartered an entire P & O liner for her comfort. On her arrival in Bombay she found an entire train fitted out with luxurious interiors to take her, its sole passenger, up to the maharajah's wedding-cake-like palace in Kapurthala that was fashioned after the palace at Versailles.

Princely India was the vision splendid. From the princes' royal ateliers came the finest flowering of Indian painting, sculpture, textile, dance, architecture and music. Without royal patrons, the artistic heritage of India would never have flourished so extensively.

To dismiss the princes as merely concupiscent hedonists is to do them an injustice. Many were able and humanitarian rulers. Nawab Taley Khan of Palanpur confided to a fellow ruler that though he personally was sorry to see the dissolution of his princely state, he was happy because it was in the best interests of the people. Today, many of the princes' elderly retainers, too enfeebled to work, still draw salaries from their mai-baap, their mother and father.

In 1970, Prime Minister Indira Gandhi derecognized the princes and withdrew their life pensions that had been enshrined in the Indian Constitution. Though the princes now belong to the past, their memory lingers on in the popular imagination.

BAMBA MULLER

married Maharajah Duleep Singh of the Punjab,
fifth king of Lahore

ADA DOUGLAS WETHERILL

married Maharajah Duleep Singh

Bamba Muller was born on 6 July 1848, the illegitimate daughter of Ludwig Muller, a partner in the German firm of merchant bankers Todd, Muller and Company, and a respected figure in Alexandria's cosmopolitan society. Bamba's mother, a beautiful young Abyssinian named Sofia, was bought by a German merchant at the Cairo slave market. He had intended to return her to Abyssinia, but died before he was able to do so. Just before dying he asked his friend Ludwig Muller to look after her and Ludwig took her as his mistress. In due course, Ludwig had placed Bamba, their daughter, in the care of the American mission in Cairo. And it was here, at the mission school, that Bamba met the prince who became her husband.

In 1849, following the death of Maharajah Ranjit Singh, known as 'The Lion of the Punjab' for his great success as a warrior, the Punjab region was in turmoil with various factions fighting over who should become maharajah. The British used this as an excuse to seize the eighty thousand square mile principality, ransack the palace in Lahore and bring Duleep Singh, the eleven-year-old heir, to England. Their aim was to

Bamba Muller

bring him under their control so that he would not rally the Sikhs behind him and become a threat to British rule.

Born in 1838, Duleep was the fourth son of Ranjit Singh and his third wife, Rani Jindan Kaur, a dancer who was the daughter of a palace doorkeeper. By this time Ranjit Singh was elderly and unwell, and it was widely thought that Jindan Kaur was simply passing off the child of one of her lowly young lovers as the ageing lion's progeny.

Among the many treasures the British came away with from Lahore was the legendary Koh-i-noor diamond, Ranjit Singh's prized possession. Given to Queen Victoria, it surpassed even the nizam of Hyderabad's Jacob diamond. (On one occasion Queen Victoria had tactlessly shown the Koh-i-noor to Duleep to admire, forgetting that it had belonged to his father.) In exchange for Duleep's bountiful state and the peerless diamond, the British bestowed a forty thousand pound annuity upon the young maharajah. Under Victoria's watchful eye he was put in the care of a guardian, Dr John Login, a dour Scotsman who was a surgeon in the Bengal army, and brought up a Christian and an English gentleman. His portrait was painted by Winterhalter and he was taught to dance.

Duleep's Punjab – Jind, Kapurthala and Patiala – and its Sikh rulers had remained steadfast allies of the British during the Indian Mutiny of 1857. They prospered for their loyalty, being awarded lands in Oudh from which they drew revenue. The British were prepared to turn a blind eye to misbehaviour by them that in other states would have ensured annexation.

Duleep had wanted to marry a woman of 'unblemished' European heritage — Sir John Login's niece — but because he was Indian this had been out of the question. Queen Victoria felt that her goddaughter Princess Gouramma, daughter of the rajah of Coorg, might make Duleep a suitable wife, and overtures were made to the rajah when Duleep was sixteen and the princess thirteen. While Duleep liked the girl, he was not attracted to her, so nothing became of the plan. (Some time later, the princess formed relationships with a stable boy and an under butler and Queen Victoria described her as 'overexcitable'. A marriage was hastily arranged between Gouramma and Colonel John Campbell, Lady Login's brother — Gouramma's senior by thirty-three years. She died aged twenty-three.)

At about this time, Duleep's mother died, as did Sir John Login. These deaths precipitated Duleep's search for a wife. On 16 February 1864 he left England taking Rani Jindan's body (encased in a coffin lined with lead) back to India to be cremated according to Sikh funeral rites. En route, he stopped at Cairo, where he visited the American Presbyterian Mission. Here he was much taken with a young student teacher struggling to control a large, unruly class, their din drowning out her soft voice. His favourable first impressions were reinforced when he saw her at the school prizegiving. This girl was Bamba Muller, and he was assured by the mission that she would make him a good wife.

Slightly built and graceful, Bamba was described by those who knew her as interesting rather than handsome, though Duleep thought her pretty. (According to him, the name Bamba meant 'pink'.) She had a sweet nature, was self-possessed, even-tempered and had a natural dignity. She was shy and socially inept, however, probably because she was embarrassed by her illegitimacy. The fact that she only spoke Arabic would also have distanced her from 'respectable' society — the class of people to which her father belonged.

Duleep told Bamba he loved her and asked her to be his wife, but she did not understand. An interpreter was summoned and when Bamba realized the nature of Duleep's request she gave him an embroidered handkerchief. Duleep gave her a ring and a pair of earrings and then continued on to India to have his mother's body cremated in Bombay and her ashes scattered on the Godavari River.

Bamba's father, Ludwig Muller, was opposed to the marriage and prophesied that it would end unhappily, but her mother Sofia was in favour. She insisted that Bamba tell Duleep of her illegitimacy, and the story goes that Duleep said he could hardly object, being a child of his father's third wife.

While Duleep was in India the mission carried out his instructions and Bamba was given English and music lessons and intensive domestic training. He also requested that she be given two maids so she could become accustomed to giving orders. In a letter to Mrs Dales, wife of the head of the mission, Duleep wrote:

> I know how dearly you love Bamba, it is natural you should feel pangs at the thought of losing her. I sympathise with you cordially but you must pardon my selfishness in being delighted at the hope of possessing that Precious Pearl which is invaluable to me. I feel I am not worthy of her. She is such a spiritually minded girl – it will indeed be a source of great pleasure to me to secure her happiness in every way.

On 9 June Duleep was back in Egypt and he and Bamba were married in a civil ceremony at the British consulate in Alexandria in the presence of a handful of witnesses. He was twenty-four and she fifteen. Duleep wore European clothes, save for a red tarboosh, while Bamba wore a traditional European bridal dress of antique white moiré with a fichu of point d'Alencon and short lace sleeves. She had orange blossoms in her hair pinning her gauze veil, a string of fine pearls round her neck and wore a bracelet set with diamonds. A religious ceremony was then performed by an American minister at Ludwig Muller's house, at Ramleh, a few miles from Alexandria.

Bamba and Duleep spent a month at Ludwig Muller's house, then enjoyed a second, more lavish honeymoon at Claridges Hotel in London, and a trip to Scotland.

Living in India was never an option for Duleep as the British had ruled that he should not be allowed to set up a home there, in case he became a focus for anti-imperial sentiment. In September of that year he settled on a marital home, buying Elveden Hall in Suffolk for £105,000. He had the Georgian country house rebuilt and the interior designed to resemble an Indian palace with marble walls, stars painted on the ceilings, scalloped arches and mosaic floors. The library walls were lined with gold-embroidered Kashmiri shawls. Indian servants saw to Duleep and Bamba's every need, and for diversion there were birds of prey in the mews, kangaroos in the garden and apes in the kitchen garden. Duleep, as befitting an English gentleman, had been brought up to have a love of field sports and the shooting on the seventeen-thousand-acre estate was among the best in the country. Over the years it attracted many famous guests, including the Prince of Wales. One season the bag was ninety-six hundred pheasants and ninety-four hundred partridges.

Before Bamba came out in society a governess was appointed to teach her English, and Duleep encouraged her to dress fashionably in the English style. He insisted, however, that her skirts were cut short and that she wear a large amount of jewellery, so a style was settled upon that was 'daring faux-Egyptian'.

Everyone who met Bamba found her modest and quiet. Lady Sophia Leven, a friend of the family, wrote that when Bamba was asked whether she would like to do something or

Bamba Muller

not, she would answer, 'Maharajah wish — I wish.' Soon after
the marriage Bamba became pregnant, but the boy died a day
after he was born.

In December 1865 Duleep and Bamba were invited by
Queen Victoria to have dinner and spend the night at Windsor
Castle. The queen and the princesses warmed to Bamba and
when the couple's second child, Prince Victor Albert, was
born, Queen Victoria agreed to be his sponsor.

In the course of the next twelve years Bamba had seven
more children. She was kept busy at Elveden caring for her
young and running the household. Ever the dutiful wife, she
nevertheless had her concerns about her husband, fearing that
Duleep's 'heathenness' might come out in their children, a
characteristic that she referred to as 'the old nature'.

Duleep was a generous host and entertained at Elveden on
a grand scale but Bamba did not take easily to English social
life. She was condescended to and scarcely more than tolerated
by those in Duleep's social circle who saw her as inferior because
she was both coloured and illegitimate. Over the years Duleep
became increasingly neglectful of her and the children, and
spent much of his time squiring young actresses around Europe.
He set up Polly Ash, a chorus girl from the Alhambra Theatre,
in a luxurious flat at Covent Garden and gave her an annuity.
In Paris he shared the courtesan Leonide le Blanc with the Duc
d'Aumale and the young Clemenceau and spent much of his
time fomenting rebellion against the British government.

In 1884 Duleep left Bamba and the children at Elveden and
set up house in Kensington in London. At about this
time he met Ada Douglas Wetherill at Cox's Hotel in
Knightsbridge where she was working as a chambermaid. Ada
was born on 13 February 1869 in Kennington, Surrey, the
daughter of a chronometer maker, so at the time the couple
met she would have been fifteen or sixteen. Julian Field, in

Uncensored Recollections, wrote, 'The Prince was so much in love with her that she had to send a wire twice a day to Elveden to tell him how she was getting on.' Ada had the bearing of an aristocrat. 'But when she spoke the charm vanished. Her manners were admirable, but her voice had the unmistakable Whitechapel accent, and her pronunciation and the expressions she used were, to say the least, abnormal.' She was said to like brandy and soda with her breakfast.

On the infrequent occasions when Duleep visited Suffolk he and Bamba would have fierce rows and he would be drunk and brooding. Bamba longed for a quiet, ordered life away from the public eye, and was unable to cope with six children and an absentee husband who humiliated her through his womanizing and extravagance. She became withdrawn and introverted and was probably suffering from agoraphobia. She neglected the house, took little interest in outside events and became increasingly an object of pity. More kindly than accurately it was said that a fall upon the ice several years earlier was the cause of her erratic behaviour. Others observed that she had taken to drink 'to an injurious extent'. Duleep, with ever-mounting debts, gave notice to all the estate staff. Neglected by Bamba and Duleep, and without a nanny to care for them, the children ran wild.

For years Duleep had been living beyond his means and despite selling off numerous possessions he was being increasingly pressed by creditors. He became increasingly angry with the British government and with Queen Victoria. He claimed that he was not being paid his full pension and announced that he would reclaim what was rightfully his: the Punjab and the Koh-i-noor diamond. In private, to friends, Duleep used to refer to Queen Victoria as 'Mrs Fagin'.

In 1886, much against Ada's wishes, Duleep left England for India, taking Bamba and the children with him. He was ready to seize back the Punjab. At Aden, however, he was intercepted by Indian government officials and sent back to Europe. In the end all he managed to do to register his rebellious feelings was to cease being a Christian and become a Sikh once more.

Duleep sailed from Aden to Marseilles, and took rooms in the Grand Hotel in Paris. Bamba and the children returned to England and were initially lodged at Claridges, in London. When they could no longer afford to stay there they moved into a house in Holland Park that Duleep had bought when Elveden was mortgaged to pay off his huge debts. The London house was hardly habitable, however, as it was bare of furniture. Bamba, drinking ever more heavily, wrote despairingly to Duleep, but received no reply. Her father visited Duleep in Paris and succeeded in getting him to agree to give Bamba half the income of Elveden, plus the occasional thirty pounds. Duleep then placed a notice in *The Times* resigning all his English property to Bamba, so that all his debts became hers.

By 1887 Duleep was informing people that Bamba was giving him nothing from her allowance – the pension that Queen Victoria had managed to secure for her and the children. Meanwhile Bamba was being increasingly pressed by his creditors. The British government, for their part, were debating whether the children had the right to be called princes and princesses. It was thought that it would lead to their becoming conceited.

In the face of Bamba's complete inability to cope, Arthur Oliphant, son of Duleep's late comptroller, took over the job of raising Duleep and Bamba's offspring. He found the children had little idea of morals or manners, and they behaved like wild young animals. They had never had books, had not learnt to play any musical instruments, and had never had other children for company. Prince Victor was a wastrel, living up to the title of shahzadah, grandchild of a king, without the means of doing so. The girls did not know how to walk like young ladies or how to conduct themselves in polite society; worse, they had not been brought up with a knowledge of Christianity. In due course Arthur Oliphant moved them to his house at Folkestone where he and his wife became their foster parents.

Duleep, who now referred to himself as 'Sovereign of the Sikh Nation and Implacable Foe of the British Government', was in Paris with Ada.

The India Office was deeply concerned about Duleep's involvement with Ada. As his consort, they saw her as a threat to the empire and from the time she became involved with Duleep she was spied upon. She was a much stronger character than Bamba and yearned for power and wealth. The British believed that she was encouraging Duleep in his attempts to regain his kingdom.

In March 1887 Duleep travelled to Russia in an unsuccessful attempt to enlist the czar's support in reclaiming the Punjab. Ada accompanied Duleep, along with his manservant, two spaniels and thirteen trunks. In order to enter the country she posed as Madame Patrick Casey, wife of an Irish Republican revolutionary, and was detained for a while by the czar's gendarmes because they thought she was a circus fortune-teller. By May Ada was pregnant and was telling people that she was Duleep's wife. For years Duleep had showed no interest in his children, and he now wrote Victor telling the family to consider him dead.

By this time Bamba was 'dying of a broken heart', according to Queen Victoria. She was suffering from diabetes and depression and as the year progressed she became increasingly sick. On 16 September she died of renal failure and the following week her body was taken by special train in a 'duplex funeral car' from London to Thetford for the funeral and burial at Elveden church. Elveden estate workers were her pallbearers and the queen and the prince of Wales sent wreathes. The queen was concerned at how Bamba had been treated and promised to take care of the children.

On the day of Bamba's funeral Duleep wrote to the Elveden estate manager telling him how he was looking forward to a forthcoming hunting trip to the Caucasus and asking the manager to send him Bamba's hunting saddle which he intended Ada to use. Shortly thereafter news reached Russia that Maharani Bamba had died, and Ada's dishonesty in claiming to be Duleep's wife was exposed. The czar was incensed at Duleep's behaviour and the couple found themselves socially ostracized.

On 26 December 1887, Ada gave birth to a daughter, Pauline Alexandra, at Billoi's Hotel, a Moscow boarding house. It was midwinter and bitterly cold, and Duleep had taken to sleeping with two fierce dogs in his room and a revolver under his pillow because he feared assassination. In 1888 the couple were living in Moscow on ten shillings a day, and Duleep had resorted to selling his fine clothing in order to keep them going.

In 1889 they were back in Paris, and on 20 May they were married at the Town Hall of the huitieme arrondisement, which was considered the most fashionable place in the city to be married. By this time Ada was three months pregnant with her second child, and by French law the marriage legitimized both the baby she was carrying and the couple's other daughter, Pauline. Ada's mother had given permission for her to marry, given that she had now turned twenty, and both she and Ada's sister were present. In official British reports the women were described as 'Philistines'.

The bride wore a lavender dress and carried a bouquet of lilies-of-the-valley. Duleep was in morning dress and wore diamond-studded decorations and an emerald tie-pin. The mayor officiated at the wedding and a count and a baron were among the four witnesses who signed the register. Duleep told friends that he and Ada had been married some time earlier according to Sikh rites and that he had wanted to marry her officially for some time.

Ada gave birth to Ada Irene Beryl in Paris on 25 October 1889. Duleep had wanted to return to Russia but they had decided against going as many people there thought that Ada was an English spy. By 1890 Duleep was drinking heavily and there were reports of him falling from his carriage. According to the India Office he was encouraged by Ada to regularly visit night houses (brothels) and music halls, and she was described as vulgar and brainless. The reports claimed that Ada's only aim in life was to spend all Duleep's money, and that she decided on where they were to live according to whether or not she would be accepted there socially.

Nine months later, in mid-1890, Duleep had a stroke that paralysed his left leg and the left side of his face. The doctor who was caring for him reported 'the wife of the maharajah is lamentably deficient in the act of nursing'. Duleep, accompanied by Ada and their two daughters, took a suite at the grandest hotel in Nice, the Hotel des Anglais. His son, Victor, and Ada would leave the invalid Duleep alone, except for one servant, while they went off to gamble heavily at the casino. Duleep's health was steadily deteriorating.

In 1891 Duleep and Queen Victoria were reconciled when the queen agreed to meet him at her hotel in Grasse where she was on holiday. She would not receive Ada, however, saying that it was Ada's behaviour in living with Duleep while Bamba was alive that had made her unacceptable, rather than her profession as an actress. (It seems the queen was confusing

Ada with someone else: officials attempted to keep her in the dark regarding Duleep's 'immoral' activities.) An extremely emotional Duleep apologized to the queen for his faults and she duly forgave him.

On 22 October 1893 Duleep died in Paris from what was described as 'an apoplectic fit'. Ada was not with him at the time. Like Bamba, he was buried in the churchyard at Elveden, and estate workers carried the coffin of the absentee squire they had known as 'the Black Prince'. Queen Victoria sent her condolences to Victor but not to Ada. Her Lord-in-Waiting Lord Camoys stood in for her at Duleep's funeral and placed on his coffin a wreath made of immortelles saying 'From Queen Victoria'.

After Duleep's death Ada stayed on in Paris, and at the Battle of Verdun she drove a French Red Cross ambulance. On her return to England in 1919 she was reported to have debts worth seventeen thousand pounds. She led a quiet life in Turnbridge Wells and in her obituary *The Times* noted that she had applied for a loan to buy a hat shop. She died on 6 August 1930 and was cremated at Golders Green Crematorium. Her daughter Pauline and stepdaughter Sophia attended the funeral, but stepdaughters Catherine and Bamba refused to come. Bamba hated Ada and would tell people that she was a British spy. She blamed Ada for Duleep's downfall.

Bamba's children were without issue, as were Ada's. In 1903 Victor was before the bankruptcy court because he had accrued huge debts. The India Office withdrew his pension and he had to lie low in France. He married Lady Anne, duchess of Coventry. Frederick remained a bachelor and became a well-known Norfolk antiquary. Sophia and Catherine also never married and lived together in a grace-and-favour residence granted them by Queen Victoria. Bamba married Lt Col David

Sutherland, an Indian army doctor, and lived in Lahore. Albert, the youngest of the family, died aged fourteen. Pauline married Lt J.S. Torry who died from wounds sustained at the Battle of Loos in 1915. Ada married Pierre Marie Villament in 1926 and later drowned herself.

FLORRIE BRYAN
married Maharajah Rajendar Singh of Patiala

*A*ccording to Margaret McMillan, in *Women of the Raj*, Florrie Bryan was working as a music hall entertainer when she met Maharajah Rajendar Singh of Patiala. Records in the India Office Library suggest otherwise, however, providing evidence of what officials deemed to be the unsavoury nature of Florrie's family.

Florrie's father was head clerk of the Central Police Office in Lahore. Florrie's family, who were of Irish descent, were known as 'Lahore people'. Florrie's brother had a modest reputation with horses and was employed in 1890 for five hundred rupees a month as superintendent of the Patiala State Stables. To Patiala he brought his wife and his three young sisters. None was beautiful but Florrie was considered gentle, according to the political agent of Patiala, Lieutenant Colonel Irvine. A Mr Field, the engineer-in-charge of the Patiala Canals, agreed. He told British spies that Florrie was quiet and modest and 'the only good one out of a bad lot'.

Maharajah Rajendar Singh was renowned for his preference for the company of 'low-class European parasites'. The Bryans seemed to fit the bill perfectly. First Rajendar seduced Florrie's sister-in-law, then Florrie's elder sister. When the sister became pregnant Rajendar paid one Mr Wallace, the private secretary of the maharana of Dholpur, twenty thousand rupees to marry her. Florrie's younger sister was then taken up by the maharajah. She too became pregnant but, to the maharajah's relief, she miscarried. Florrie was the last of the sisters to succumb to the maharajah's charms and she too conceived.

It was at about this time that Florrie's brother stormed off to Florrie's apartment in a drunken state, knowing that he would find the maharajah visiting. Bryan abused Rajendar roundly for his conduct towards his three sisters and British records note that a fight was only prevented by the intervention of a group of bystanders. Spies reported to the British that the maharajah had drunk himself into such an incoherent state that eventually he had to be carried away from Florrie's room in the small hours of the morning. Given such conduct, the British government were scornful of Field's assessment of Florrie's character and 'questioned the morals of a girl who would marry the abuser of her own sister'.

Patiala was a rich state, drawing its revenue from six thousand square miles of fertile agricultural land in the Punjab, the granary of India. Rajendar Singh was born in 1872 and had assumed the throne in 1876 as a minor after his father, Maharajah Mohinder Singh, had died at the age of twenty-four under suspicious circumstances.

It was probably Florrie's quiet malleability that led to her becoming Rajendar Singh's wife. British officials noted that the 'maharajah had fancied her for two years' before she became his mistress. Despite his womanizing ways, it seems Rajendar genuinely cared for her. He put out feelers through his friend Lord Beresford to see if Lord Lansdowne, the viceroy, would assent to his marriage to Florrie. Not surprisingly, permission was refused, but Rajendar married her in secret anyway.

On 8 April 1893, when she was five months pregnant, Florrie was baptized according to the Sikh religion. After the ritual, wearing traditional Jatni dress and 'native jewellery', she was married to the maharajah in both Hindu and Sikh ceremonies. Her name was changed to Harman Kaur.

News of the marriage quickly spread through the bazaar and when Florrie and Rajendar arrived at the railway station to catch a train to Dholpur, where they intended to spend their honeymoon, a large crowd had gathered to see the new bride.

Rajendar's First Her Highness, his principal maharani and mother of his two-year-old son Bhupinder, was desolate when she heard of the marriage. Rajendar banished her to the fort where she cried 'day and night'. (She eventually died of loneliness, neglect and the slow debilitating effects of tuberculosis.) His other relatives were no less distressed, fearing that Florrie's soon-to-be-born child might prevent Bhupinder from being first in succession. The British were no more in favour of the marriage than the maharajah's family. When Rajendar notified the government that his marriage was a fait accompli, the Resident declared the marriage 'will render your position both with Europeans and Indians most embarrassing'.

Officially the British did not acknowledge the marriage in any way. Files note they preferred not to raise the question of recognition, thinking that it would be unlikely for Florrie to accompany the maharajah on any state or semi-state occasion in any case. Even unoffically, Florrie was not welcomed by the British. When the heat of the plains became too intense she went to Mussoorie, and not to the more pukka hill station of Simla.

Florrie's love for the maharajah and his infatuation with her suited Florrie's disorderly and impecunious family. Despite the fact that she would never be socially accepted by the Raj, her position as Rajendar's wife offered them social mobility and thus economic opportunity.

Initially Florrie managed to keep Rajendar in some sort of check, but basically his life was devoted to wine, women and sport. When British advisers complained that he was not spending enough time on administrative work he told them that he was not prepared to spend more than one-and-a-half hours a day on running the state.

He was willing, however, to spend eight hours a day on horseback. A typical day was spent in the following way:

> riding in the morning to pig stick
> 11 a.m. Patiala pegs, double strength at the club
> game of rackets
> sign a few letters
> polo
> roller-skating
> dinner

Rajendar was fanatical about sports, preferring horses to humans. He had three stables in Patiala in which he maintained seven hundred of the best thoroughbreds in India. He was a first-class polo player and his team, 'The Patiala Tigers', which carried a handicap of forty, was the best polo team in India.

Cricket was another love: he was the first Indian member of the MCC and the first maharajah to engage English cricket professionals to coach in Patiala. He discovered and encouraged the talents of Ranjitsinhji, the Indian prince who later played gloriously for England and took her to victory against Australia in 1900. Rajendar recruited 'Ranji' to the Patiala team and made him his aide-de-camp.

In Calcutta Rajendar owned a magnificent mansion called Granville. Along the Mall in Simla he was the proud owner of three magnificent residences: Cedars, Rookwood and Oakover. From the balcony of Oakover you could glimpse the Himalayas through banks of deodar and flowering rhododendron. Once Rajendar's son Bhupinder disgraced himself in Simla – he persuaded Lady Curzon, when she was dining with him and several other princes, to dress up in Indian clothes. Lord Curzon was not present at the time, and when the story leaked out it caused a sensation. Unfazed, Rajendar simply built himself a sumptuous new residence at Chail, forty miles away. He had the top cut off a nearby mountain and had a cricket pitch constructed, the highest in the world, which is still in use today.

Even by the spendthrift standards of the princes, Rajendar was exceptional. He reportedly sauntered into a shop of a electrical furnishing firm in Calcutta and, miffed at not being recognized, decided to leave an unforgettable impression. He asked the price of the contents of the shop and was told it came to sixty thousand pounds. 'Very well,' he replied. 'Send them along.'

Rajendar imported the first motor car to India in 1892, a French Deboin Bouton with the number plate Patiala 0. It travelled at a sedate fifteen kilometres an hour and was of great fascination to his subjects.

More than cars or palaces, Rajendar was noted for his collection of jewels. Though he gave a modest amount of jewellery to Florrie, he reserved most of his jewels for himself. He owned a breastplate and tiara of emeralds which was hung with loops of diamonds and pearls, a diamond necklace that belonged to Empress Eugenie and that originated with the British Crown jewels when James II took them with him to France, a three-row pearl collar, diamond star pins, and count-less less valuable pieces. In 1899 Mary Curzon wrote to her parents from Calcutta describing Maharajah Rajendar Singh in full regalia:

> The glittering array of guests included the great Maharajahs of Patiala, Scindia of Gwalior, Kashmir — in magnificent jewels — Number I [Patiala] had

a breastplate of enormous diamonds and necklace after necklace of pearls.

Collins and Lapierre sketched a portrait in exact same regalia:

> Centrepiece of the great collection of the Sikh Maharaja of Patiala was a pearl necklace insured by Lloyds of London for one million dollars. Its most intriguing item, however, was a diamond breastplate, its luminous surface composed of 1001 brilliantly matched blue-white diamonds. Until the end of the century, it had been the custom of the Maharaja of Patiala to appear once a year before his subjects naked except for his diamond breastplate, his organ in full and glorious erection. His performance was judged a kind of temporal manifestation of the Shivalinga, the phallic representation of Lord Shiva's organ. As the Maharaja walked about, his subjects gleefully applauded, their cheers acknowledging both the dimensions of the princely organ and the fact that it was supposed to be radiating magic powers to drive away evil spirits from the land.

The writer Rudyard Kipling visited Patiala's Baradi Palace and was much impressed. It covered eleven acres and had bedrooms like reception rooms, bathrooms like ballrooms and vast gardens dotted with ivory pavilions. There were 15 dining rooms, 143 cooks, 17 of whom only cooked curries, and there was a silver dinner service that in 1930 was conservatively valued at thirty thousand pounds. Maharani Florrie had the pleasure of sharing with her husband the dubious comfort of a gold-plated bed.

Florrie existed in a peculiar no-woman's world (not uncommon for the European wives of princes) where she was neither accepted by her own kind, because of her low class and her imprudent choice of husband, nor welcomed by the maharajah's family and subjects. Lieutenant Colonel Irvine sympathized with her predicament, noting how lonely she was and commenting on the contempt with which she was viewed by ladies of Patiala's official community. He wrote in his memoirs that even European visitors to Patiala did not pay her the attention she was due as their hostess: 'Often after dinner she would sit lonely and neglected in the drawing room.'

Florrie had conceived five months before coming to live at the palace, so her first experience of zenana life was celebratory. She was massaged and hennaed; her hair was oiled and plaited and dressed in fragrant flowers; and she was draped in the finest silk brocades. As she entered the final months of pregnancy she luxuriated in the lavish comfort of the zenana. Cool pools of water and heavy silk punkahs kept the heat at bay until she was finally delivered of what the British spoke dismissively of as a 'five months' child. The Indians were no less contemptuous. Rumours began to circulate, almost certainly begun by Rajendar's Indian maharani, that the child had been bought in the bazaars of Hissar.

The new baby consumed much of Florrie's time. She played with him, bathed and dressed him, but as was the custom, she engaged a wet nurse to feed him. At the age of seven months, her robust little boy became sick, losing weight and lying listlessly in his cot. Before there was time for Florrie to call in a government doctor the child was dead, and with India's heat his body had to be disposed of quickly. There was no time for a postmortem, but Florrie was certain her baby had been murdered by the zenana women acting under the orders of First Her Highness. Florrie believed the wet nurse was to blame. It would have been easy for her to rub a lethal dose of opium onto her nipples before the child suckled. There was no evidence and Florrie knew India well enough to know that she was not going to get any.

First Her Highness had secured her son's position for a while, but with Florrie alive there was always the chance she would produce another child. The only permanent solution was to get rid of Florrie.

Florrie became deeply depressed. She had no one to comfort her. She had tried to distance herself from her reprobate family upon her marriage but no respectable European was willing to associate with her. Rajendar was getting deeper into debt and drinking ever more heavily. More and more 'white trash', pimps and con men flocked to Patiala, attracted by the rich pickings offered by a weak, alcoholic prince. Florrie tried to caution Rajendar against his so-called friends who were only too happy to encourage his dissipated habits.

Within two years of her son's death, Florrie too, lay dying of mysterious causes. Her nurse told Lieutenant Colonel Irvine that Rajendar covered her bed 'with jewellery, musical boxes, mechanical toys — with everything a devoted husband could think of to distract her mind from illness'. Guilt probably also prompted Rajendar to behave in such a way, for he had taken to consorting with an eager group of opportunistic women — the wives of various Europeans whom he employed in Patiala. The British described how he

> disported with women of dubious character at his house "Granville" in Calcutta. They got him to buy them jewellery. Florrie's body was racked by a real physical ailment but it was the sickness that assailed her spirit that was the real agent of her destruction.

Though he arranged for hundred pure white peacocks to be sacrificed on Florrie's death, it was little compensation for a life of rejection and neglect. Soon after Florrie's death Rajendar gave her jewels to his best friend, the maharana of Dholpur. He told British authorities that it had been Florrie's dying wish that he should do so, but subsequent investigations revealed that he owed Dholpur a great deal of money.

Five years after Florrie's death Rajendar died at the age of twenty-seven. The viceroy, Lord Curzon, writing to Edward VII about Rajendar, said that the maharajah had finally succumbed to delirium tremens, and not a horse riding accident as had been popularly reported.

OLIVE MONOLESCUE

married Ranbir Singh, maharajah of Jind

Olive Monolescue was a Roman Catholic of Anglo-Romanian origin whose maternal grandfather was a pensioned conductor of the ordinance department. He and his wife had retired to Poona.

Olive's mother, Lizzie Coleman, married a Mr Monolescue, a barber who owned a shop in Meadows Street, the Fort, Bombay. Lizzie Coleman had four children with Monolescue, of whom Olive and a son named Eugene survived. Monolescue eventually deserted Lizzie, who took up a job with the Bombay Telephone Company and then worked for De Silva's Circulating Library. It was while she was working as a governess in 1896 that Lizzie met Park Van Tassell, variously employed as a balloonist and a strolling performer, who was 'known to the police'.

Of Dutch origin, Park Van Tassell had married American Edith Nowland in Calcutta's Bankipore in 1892. Park and Edith had two sons and then she returned to America. By 1899, Edith was back in Asia working as a barmaid in the Royal Hotel, Rangoon. There she met and married a friend of Van Tassell's, a boxer named Brophy. While Edith was to-ing and fro-ing between the US and Asia, Park joined up with Lizzie and they travelled through north India giving balloon demonstrations.

Park, Lizzie and Olive were visiting the Garhwal Hills, south-east of Simla, where Park had arranged to give a ballooning

and cinematograph display at Maler Kotla. At that time the
political agent Colonel Melliss was inspecting Jind and the
relief of Ladysmith in South Africa had just taken place.
Ranbir Singh, maharajah of Jind, heard of Park's show and
thought it would be a good way to honour the military victory,
so he invited Park across to Mussoorie. As soon as Ranbir
Singh saw Olive he was smitten, as was his great friend
Maharajah Gopal Narain Singh.

Ranbir Singh was born in 1881 and succeeded as a minor
to his thirteen hundred-square-mile state which enjoyed a
thirteen-gun salute. He had no interest whatever in politics
and left the running of his state to his prime minister. Reserved
and deaf, his great interest was dogs and he had the best
kennels in India. He held a Dog Week every year which the
British bemoaned as it not only attracted dog-fanciers from
all over India but also numerous disreputable characters who
were more anxious to enjoy Ranbir's lavish hospitality than
to show their dogs. By 1900 Ranbir had two Sikh wives,
Dhelma and Gurcharan Kaur.

Ranbir's father Raghbir Singh had been known for his
eccentricities rather than for his administrative capabilities.
He had his own Highland band kitted out in full kilt and
pipes, the pipers wearing pink cotton tights to hide their dusky
knees. Raghbir was an indulgent parent who spent a fortune
on photographs of Ranbir and on importing Parisian scents
and essences for his daily bath.

Ranbir was so taken with Olive that he devised a scheme
to get Park and his family across to Sangrur, his capital, where
they would be more susceptible to his wishes. Park gave his
balloon demonstration to celebrate Ranbir's birthday, which
coincided with the Hindu festival of Dusserah. Ranbir had,
in the meantime, briefed his procurer of women, Sardar Atari,
to enter into negotiations to obtain Olive for him as a wife.

*Olive Monolescue and her husband
Ranbir Singh, maharajah of Jind*

Park and Lizzie offered Atari a percentage of the money they hoped to receive in order that he should persuade Ranbir to increase the amount he was prepared to pay for Olive. The Punjab's lieutenant-governor discovered that Atari was playing one side against the other and ordered him to leave Jind. Negotiations continued, however, and terms were finally agreed, with Lizzie and Park signing Olive away for fifty thousand rupees.

The agreement noted that Lizzie could stay in Sangrur as long as she wished and that Park could visit them both whenever he liked; Olive could wear her own Western style clothes; she was to receive a thousand rupees a month as pocket money; Ranbir could visit his two Sikh maharanis but he was to dismiss prostitutes and nautch girls and was not to marry any native woman or take prostitutes in Olive's lifetime; Olive and Ranbir's first male child was to receive twenty-five thousand rupees yearly, their second twelve thousand rupees and the third six thousand rupees yearly; and, finally, Olive was to have her own private carriage, her own servants and a Christian nurse.

Though the amount of fifty thousand rupees was ostensibly for Olive's benefit, Lizzie had retained the right to have it deposited in any bank she nominated. The British learned of the unsavoury deal and tried to intervene, but Lizzie made off with the money.

It seems that after Lizzie and Park had married Olive off, Lizzie decided that procuring women for Indian princes was an easy and rewarding way to make a living. In 1901 police reports cited her as travelling to the Punjab along with her young niece Florrie Coleman. Florrie had become fed up with the low pay she received at Badham Pile and Company in Bombay and had readily agreed to be married to a wealthy Jind noble. Lizzie and Park had teamed up with Sardar Atari:

he would provide the men and the money while Lizzie and Park provided the girls. In time, however, Lizzie and Park split up. Having made her fortune as a pimp and no longer prepared to tolerate Park's womanizing, Lizzie remarried and went to live in Europe.

In 1900, Olive and Ranbir were married in his private apartments in his palace at Sangrur. Olive became a convert to Sikhism, which allows converts from Christianity or Islam for the purpose of marriage, and was given the Sikh name Jaswant Kaur.

For his negligence in preventing the marriage and the illegal appropriation of monies paid by the maharajah, the political agent, Lieutenant Colonel Irvine, was removed from his post by a furious Viceroy Lord Curzon, who had been told by Ranbir that the marriage was none of his business. Curzon was not a man to cross. It was decreed by the British that Olive was not to hold the title 'Maharanee or Maharanee of Jind'.

Olive conceived soon after marriage and gave birth to a son on 12 September 1901. But six months later, in almost identical circumstances to those of Florrie Bryan's son, Olive's child died. Not long after, Olive gave birth to a daughter, but by this time she and Ranbir were having serious differences and he had turned his attention once more to his courtesans and an endless stream of prostitutes. One prostitute, a Muslim girl, bore him a son and it was this child that Ranbir eventually pushed to have recognized as his heir. Despite the mother's occupation and the child's illegitimate status, the British were inclined to agree to Ranbir's wishes. And yet Olive, whose social position was no less than that of Ranbir's Muslim paramour, was not allowed to appear in polite society. In 1901 she and Ranbir had been refused permission to visit Simla — a lesson for Ranbir that British wishes were not to be taken lightly. The foreign internal proceedings of the Government

of India noted that Ranbir Singh of Jind and his wife Olive
had been denied the privilege of attending a polo tournament
in Simla for

> ... the Government of India to allow him to come
> up to Simla to amuse himself is rather to condone
> his folly. It will probably do the young man good
> to learn in the practical form of refusal of permis-
> sion to come to Simla, that the Government of
> India is displeased with him.

Olive was never officially recognized and thus never invited
to any official function. No memsahib would have dared to
invite her for tea or to join a charity event. Like Florrie, Olive
was put firmly in her place and made to feel the full brunt
of British disapproval.

At first Olive contented herself with travel. She made her
way between Europe and India on a regular basis, as did most
of the maharajahs and their European wives. While France was
a favourite haunt for many of the princes' European wives,
Olive felt ill-at-ease in the snobbish society of Cannes. She
was not interested in making a reputation for herself as an
elegant dresser or as a society hostess.

Ranbir and Olive maintained the outward form of their
marriage for twenty-eight years, but in 1928 Olive told Ranbir
she wanted a divorce. Worried about her financial security, she
asked the British to intervene and secure an annuity for her.
The British agreed to mediate, considering Ranbir's settlement
of fifteen thousand rupees annually liberal, given her humble
origins. However, Ranbir did stipulate that it was only to
continue as long as Olive led a chaste life and did not remarry.
She and her daughter Dorothy settled down in a beautiful
house in London – 9 Walpole Gardens, Chiswick – and set

up her own salon of interesting if not wholly respectable visitors. According to Dhelma, Ranbir's daughter from one of his Sikh wives, Dorothy, later committed suicide. Olive, who was said to be 'not good with money', lived till her eighties.

ANITA DELGADO

married Maharajah Jagatjit Singh of Kapurthala

EUGENIE GROSUPOVA

married Maharajah Jagatjit Singh of Kapurthala

*A*nita Delgado was performing with her sister at the New Central-Kursaal, a modern theatre in Madrid, when Maharajah Jagatjit Singh of Kapurthala saw her for the first time. The girls, who called themselves the Camellia sisters, were not professional dancers, but they were hired as curtain-raisers because of their youthful beauty and soon became favourites with the clientele — mainly intellectuals and bohemian artists. It was May 1906 and Jagatjit was visiting Spain for the wedding of King Alfonso XIII of Spain and Princess Victoria Eugenie of Battenburg. He and a number of other guests had gone to the theatre to sample some local entertainment. Jagatjit had a passion for women and as soon as he saw the beautiful sixteen-year-old Anita he fell for her.

Anita's family was not well off. Her father had run a café in Malaga, which earned the family a living because of the gambling that took place on the first floor. When the government prohibited gambling, the café became a mere coffee shop and the family emigrated to Madrid, but her father was unable to find a job.

Anita was strictly chaperoned at the theatre, so Jagatjit was unable to speak to her. He sent someone to Anita's family,

Anita Delgado

offering them money if they would allow her to come with him to Paris. Anita was indignant. Being unable to write herself, she arranged for someone to reply to the maharajah saying that she was certainly not to be bought. The correspondence continued, however, and in Jagatjit's third letter he proposed marriage, along with an offer of a hundred thousand pounds to be paid to Anita's father. The family agreed to the offer, and in August the whole family moved to Paris.

Jagatjit was born in 1872, succeeded to the throne as a minor in 1877 and attained full ruling powers in 1890. The Kapurthala family could trace its lineage back nine hundred years to Rana Kapur, a member of the Rajput ruling dynasty of Jaisalmer. A Punjab state, Kapurthala drew most of its revenue from rich lands in Oudh awarded by the British for Kapurthala's loyalty during the Indian Mutiny. Jagatjit was a larger-than-life figure, a man accustomed to authority and a leader among the Indian princes. Though only a relatively minor state, its ruler's character gave Kapurthala a significance in the public imagination that far outstripped its relative importance.

The maharajah was an inveterate traveller and wrote tracts describing his adventures abroad. An avowed Francophile, he modelled his palaces on French chateaus, filling them with French furniture and tapestries and ensuring that his progeny and their partners had as French an upbringing as possible. Variously known as the 'Emerald King', 'The richest man in the world' and 'an Asiatic Maecenas', he owned twelve palaces, including the famous sugar-pink palace in Kapurthala, modelled after Versailles, which he built for Anita and which was completed in 1909. Some say Jagatjit's palace surpassed the original in ornamentation and precious interiors.

Like most of his fellow princes, Jagatjit was an avid collector of decorations and revelled in the pomp and ceremony at which the Raj excelled. Jagatjit was sweetened by the British conferring on him honorary military titles – the GCSI and the GCIE, the raising of his salute from eleven guns to thirteen. He also received the order of the Grand Cordon of the Nile from the King of Egypt and the Grand Officier de la Legion d'Honneur from the French.

Jagatjit was a loyal subject. The Kapurthala Imperial Service Regiment served with distinction in East Africa and Mesopotamia and in the Third Afghan War. Jagatjit contributed handsomely to both the First and Second World Wars and was a member of the Indian delegation to the League of Nations Assembly at Geneva in 1926, 1927 and 1929. He was also a member of the Round Table Conference in London in 1931 at which Gandhi was present.

The British were not impressed, however, when Jagatjit and his son Paramjit attended Italian army manoeuvres in 1935 and met with Benito Mussolini. Then, to make matters worse, Jagatjit attended the Nazi Parteitag at Nuremburg. His flirtation with fascism and the agrarian clashes and communal riots that regularly took place in Kapurthala would have undone a less popular prince, but were forgiven by the British because they believed they could 'rely on Jagatjit to behave as a gentleman'.

In 1886, at the age of fourteen, Jagatjit had married the daughter of Mian Ranjit Singh of Guleria. After several years had passed and his wife had not conceived, questions were asked. Jagatjit's portly girth was blamed for his inability to consummate the marriage. According to John Lord, experts were consulted and a ramp-like bed was constructed. This solved the couple's difficulties and in due course Paramjit Singh was conceived. The invention won its happy engineer a life pension.

An enthusiastic patron of Cartier, Jagatjit commissioned him to combine the Kapurthala turban ornaments – no less than three thousand emeralds, along with circular and rose-cut diamonds, and pearls – into a crown. Jagatjit was impressed with Cartier's handiwork, observing, 'When I reach the Ritz I always wear my emerald turban jewel and my pearls. They are simply a great work of art.'

Once the Delgado family was installed in Paris, Anita's education began. She was to be turned into a young woman with all the accomplishments necessary to be a maharani. During the rest of 1906 and for most of 1907 she was educated in Paris, Brussels and London. She learned to speak French and English. She learned to dance, to play tennis, to horseback ride, to play the piano, to paint and to play billiards. In October 1907, she travelled to India, and on 28 January 1908 she and Jagatjit were married according to Sikh Anand rites. Anita was given the name Prem Kaur. She was Jagatjit's sixth wife.

In her diary, Anita described being dressed for her wedding. Two ladies-in-waiting of her mother-in-law's attended her, massaging her with perfumed oils and then dressing her in a fine white silk sari. She wore a gauzy poppy-coloured jacket embroidered in gold, with pearl buttons, and red embroidered slip-on shoes. It took two hours for her to be dressed, and the many little pleats at the front of her sari were held in place solely by a silver brooch. Anita had been hoping to wear a European-style wedding dress but when she saw herself in the mirror she was delighted with her appearance, despite the fact that she was afraid to move because she thought the sari might come apart.

Kapurthala was a fairytale for Anita. She was surrounded by luxuries and European comforts. Jagatjit treated her with great respect and kindness and she grew to love him. Jagatjit had a palace built for her, as he had for each of his European wives and mistresses. Anita's was like a miniature Versailles.

(One of these mistresses, Germain Pelligreno, Jagatjit would meet at a fashion show in Cannes when she was seventeen and he fifty-five. He hired an ocean liner to bring her out to India, then at Bombay there was an entire train waiting to transport her to Kapurthala. He also had a Moroccan girlfriend for whom he had a mosque built in Kapurthala.) Anita's palace was furnished with French furniture, Aubusson carpets, and paintings that had once hung in the finest French salons. Her dinner service was solid gold.

Jagatjit's family was appalled by the marriage. They despised Anita not only for being foreign but for her lowly origins. As a dancer she was considered akin to a prostitute. Brinda, Paramjit's wife, refused to meet Anita, dismissing her contemptuously as 'that Spanish dancer', but Anita could not have cared less.

On 26 April 1908, not long after she became Jagatjit's wife, Anita gave birth to a son, Ajit Singh. The birth was a difficult one, during which both Anita's life and her baby's were at risk.

While Anita had all the luxuries money could buy, she had no official recognition. She was simply to be referred to as the 'Spanish wife of H.H. the Maharajah of Kapurthala'. (Later the viceroy magnaminously decreed that all officials except himself could refer to Anita as 'the Spanish Rani'.) Senior officials were forbidden to meet her either on official or unofficial occasions, but officials of lower status were allowed to meet her informally. Lord Carmichael, the governor of Bengal, was severely reprimanded for introducing her to his wife at the Calcutta races and inviting her to Government House. The British government disapproved of Anita's antecedents. They were relieved that problems regarding the succession were unlikely to arise from Anita's child as the maharajah already had four sons senior to Anita's — from his Indian wives.

Anita Delgado, the 'Spanish rani'

The wife of Sir Michael O'Dwyer, the governor of the Punjab, refused to meet Anita, but at a governor's reception for the Punjab princes they met by accident. Anita had been permitted to attend the function but had been manoeveured into an alcove that was hidden by a screen of potted plants. The idea was to keep her out of official view. When Lady Dwyer became curious about the unusual looking woman in the corner, she found to her dismay it was the infamous Spanish maharani. Lady Dwyer was so shocked she blushed and fumbled a curtsey, much to Anita's delight.

Anita captured everyone's imagination. Her 'lustrous black hair reflected the gleam of a thousand lights and her sparkling dark eyes shone even brighter'. Even Princess Ourmila, daughter of Anita's foe, Brinda, described her as very beautiful 'in a dark Spanish way'. Photographer Raja Deen Dayal caught Anita on film, dressed in a sari and luxuriating in the zenana of her palace in Kapurthala. All the traditional appurterances of a woman in purdah are arranged around her: a make-up box containing the cosmetics, richly woven carpets to sit on, plump cushions and lacquer screens. Anita could easily have passed for an aristocratic Indian wife.

In fact, Anita was never required to live in the zenana, and unlike many other European women she was not intimidated by the women of the zenana. She generally wore European clothes, and she would accompany Jagatjit on his travels. She said that the first few years of her marriage were the happiest years of her life.

According to Anita's nephew, Prince Martand Singh, the hugely rich but miserly nizam of Hyderabad fell for her. When she and Jagatjit were visiting Hyderabad the nizam sent her a note telling her to unfold her dinner napkin carefully. Out fell an emerald crescent headpiece, an emerald ring and earrings. Later, the ring was crushed up by servants and used as green sprinkles on a cake. The crescent was sold and later she tried to sell the earrings and found the emeralds were fake. A portrait of Anita wearing nothing but the emerald headpiece was burned by her step-grandson, the present Maharajah Sukhjit Singh.

As Simla was for the British, so Mussoorie was for the princes, and Anita and Jagatjit would spend the hot summer months there, escaping the heat. Barbara Crossette writes in *The Great Hill Stations of Asia* that Mussoorie was created for pleasure not work. Born liberated, it quickly embraced promiscuity. She says that in the lore that accumulated around Mussoorie,

> ... was the story about how the Savoy Hotel, the Ritz
> of the mountains, rang a bell just before dawn to
> prepare the religious for prayer and chase the others
> back to their own beds before the sun came up.

One of the most popular events in Mussoorie, apparently, was a trial in virility for which a prince annually presented the winner's cup. Nine times out of ten the winner was the maharajah of Patiala.

Mussoorie nestled at almost seven thousand feet in the Garhwal Himalayas. It had farms, two breweries, hotels, a polo ground, a race course, English shops, the Evelyn Hall Nursing Home, the Happy Valley Club and the Himalaya Club. Dane Kennedy writes that from the earliest it 'was deemed an eligible residence for native princes'. And so the princely pleasure domes grew in number. Foremost was Jagatjit's Chateau de Kapurthala.

Jarmani Dass, Jagatjit's secretary, first came in contact with Jagatjit and Anita when he was invited to spend a few days at the chateau. Dass describes it as 'a very fine piece of architecture with beautiful turrets in the style of the French chateaus owned by the aristocracy of France'. He admired its 'spacious tennis court, flower gardens and rare plants overlooking the Himalayan peaks, clad in snow which shines dazzlingly on a sunny day'.

In his chateau, the maharajah played host to Mussoorie's high society:

> The Chateau de Kapurthala was the venue for the cream of society in Mussoorie during the summer season where fancy dress balls, dinners, suppers and garden parties were held three to four times a week and to which hundreds of British officers, English ladies and Indians of high society, including Maharajas and Maharanis, were invited.

At the chateau Joan Falkiner, Nancy Miller, Florrie Bryan and Margaret Elsip came together with Anita and shared their experiences as white consorts of Indian rulers. Here, they were free to wear their Western clothes and indulge in European pastimes that were frowned upon in their husbands' states.

Dass describes meeting Anita for the first time along with Jagatjit's French mistress. Both women seemed content to share each other's company.

> On the first day of my arrival at Mussoorie I was put up in 'Sunny View' – a luxurious State guest-house – and was invited to dinner by the Maharaja. At the dinner there were only six persons: the Maharaja, his Spanish Maharani named Prem Kaur whom the Maharaja married according to Sikh rites, his lady companion Mlle Louise Dujon who later married to Mr E.M. Atkinson (a tutor in Chiefs

College, Lahore), two senior household officers and myself.

Dass describes how Anita introduced him to champagne:

> When drinks were being served I was asked what I would like to drink. I replied that I would like to take lemonade. At my request the Maharani, who seemed to have a soft corner for me, asked Slawick, the Maitre d'Hotel to bring French lemonade for me. I had three glasses in all. Only later was I told that it actually was French champagne. This was how I was introduced to champagne and European way of life.

Dass soon became a regular visitor at Mussoorie. He was a keen observer, making mental notes for the books in which he and his son charted the social lives of India's princes and their consorts. He was at various times a guest of the maharajahs of Kapurthala, Patiala, Rampur, Rajpipla, Panna, Baroda, Nabha and Jind. Present in Mussoorie as well were the rulers of Tikari, Cooch Behar, Palanpur, Punjab and Indore. But none could outshine the entertainment provided by the maharajah of Kapurthala.

Fancy dress balls were the chateau's forte. Huge amounts of food and alcoholic drinks were consumed, and couples would make their way out into the chateau's large, private gardens. Couplings established in the gardens continued on the ride home in rickshaws which travelled around the

> ... Camel's Back, a circular road behind the hill facing the beautiful scenery of the high mountains, snow and perpetual greenery. Here the couples spent

hours before the women were dropped at their residences. Some bold women did not hesitate to take their lovers to their houses to share their beds.

Dass summed up Mussoorie and the hill stations generally saying, 'The whole atmosphere of these summer resorts was nothing but gaiety, frivolity and sex indulgence.' It seems that the Indian princes mimicked their British rulers in every possible way.

K.P.S. Menon tells in *Many Worlds* how Jagatjit Singh was on a visit to Rome when King Umberto of Italy called in at his hotel to pay his respects. King Umberto noticed the many photographs of beautiful women that decorated the sitting room. Jagatjit Singh had a tendency to flaunt his conquests of European women, displaying their photos as other princes mounted the heads of the tigers they had bagged. Menon writes that

> The King barked gruffly, 'Who are these women?'
> And the Maharajah replied 'They, Sir, are my wives.'
> Umberto retorted,
> 'Well I too have got as many women as you. But there's the difference between us. I don't keep 'em together. I keep 'em in different houses. You keep all yours in your palace.'

Menon writes that whether King Umberto was correct in his assessment of Jagatjit's domiciliary arrangements or not, by the time Menon reached Kapurthala the chauffeur pointed out to him the separate 'houses built for the Spanish Maharani, the French Maharani, the Georgian Maharani' and several others.

In time Anita's day as Jagatjit's favourite passed. Once described as 'a beauty who outshone all others as Venus outshines the other planets', Anita was expected to remain celibate or at least be discreet while Jagatjit moved on to new and younger mistresses and wives.

Even so Anita and Jagatjit travelled to London together, where the maharajah had his own royal suite at the Savoy Hotel. Jagatjit and Anita's bedrooms were separated by a drawing room and a passage which led to the corridor.

One night after Jagatjit had retired, Anita left her room having first made the covers seem as though she was asleep in bed. At 1.30 a.m. one of Jagatjit's senior attendants, Kushal Singh, woke his master to tell him that Anita had gone to meet her lover in the hotel.

Jagatjit went to Anita's bedroom and found her gone. He called all his officers to her room and they waited there until she returned at 3.30 a.m., her hair and clothes dishevelled. At first she told them she had gone to her maid's room because she had been unable to sleep. Jagatjit said he knew she was lying because the maid's room had been searched. Anita then said she had been with Jagatjit's diwan asking his advice, but Jagatjit had also had the diwan's room searched. He called a Colonel Enriquez to prepare separation documents, announcing that as Anita had had sexual relations with another man he wanted an immediate separation.

Anita threw herself on the floor crying. She said that she had committed no crime and that she had not been unfaithful. Jagatjit ignored her pleas and retired to his room.

Mohamed Ali Jinnah, the future president of Pakistan, who was staying with his wife in the hotel at the time, came to hear of the situation. A friend of both Jagatjit and Anita, he tried to bring about a reconciliation, telling Jagatjit he could not divorce Anita on such flimsy evidence. He said he would plead her case with the secretary of state for India.

However, accusations then followed that Anita was having an affair with Maharajkumar Mahijit Singh, Jagatjit's son from his senior maharani. When the scandal broke Mahijit threatened to kill himself, so great was the disgrace. After this Jinnah was unable to stop Jagatjit from proceeding with a divorce but he was able to secure for Anita and her handsome son Ajit Singh a large allowance.

According to Prince Martand Singh, Anita had indeed fallen in love with Mahijit Singh, and the two of them ran away together and lived in Paris. Mahijit was exiled, but later he and his father were reconciled.

Anita's account of how her marriage to Jagatjit ended differs markedly from the above version. Following a miscarriage, she became ill and was depressed. She went to Mussoorie to recover. During her long convalescence Jagatjit took a mistress, and Anita lost her privileges as the maharajah's favourite. She went to live in a house called Buena Vista, outside Kapurthala, where she became consumed by boredom and jealousy. She occupied herself with visitors, tea parties and cocktail parties and with travelling. Someone told the maharajah she had been seen horseriding at dusk with a jockey and Jagatjit became very angry. In 1925, after long discussions, Anita and Jagatjit signed a complicated and generous agreement of separation. Anita was free to leave India, and went to live in Paris. In spite of their differences, she and Jagatjit stayed in touch.

Until the outbreak of the Second World War Anita lived the life of the idle rich, with homes in Paris, Switzerland, Madrid and Malaga. She spent her summer holidays in Deauville and would visit the Lido in Venice and Nice in the winters. In the early years of the war Anita lived in Lisbon, and her son was in Buenos Aires, Argentina, as a commercial attaché. In 1941 she went to live in Madrid. In 1949 the Indian embassy in Madrid notified her of Jagatjit's death, but she was advised not to attend the funeral because the Punjab was in a sate of emergency.

Anita continued to live the life of a grand lady in her luxurious flat in Madrid. Her table was set with gold cutlery and Dresden china and she continued to wear spectacular jewels. In 1962, while awaiting the publication of her memoirs, she became gravely ill, and was cared for by her niece, Victoria. Her son was sent for, and he arrived at her bedside shortly before she died, on 7 July.

Eugenie Grosupova, Jagatjit's second European wife, was the illegitimate daughter of a Czech count and an actress, Nina Grosupova. Jagatjit met Eugenie in 1937 while she was performing at the Burga Theatre in Prague. Jagatjit may have been rich but he was no Prince Charming, and the lovely young woman was not unduly attracted to him. Eugenie's mother Nina and her grandmother Pura Grosupova felt differently – they saw Jagatjit not only as Eugenie's shining knight but as their own. One-time actresses themselves, they knew the insecurity and penury that came with the cessation of admirers in middle age. They advised Eugenie to take advantage of the circumstances, before her looks began to fade.

Eugenie took her mother and grandmother's advice and left Prague with Jagatjit, but her heart was not in the arrangement. Once they were in Kapurthala Jagatjit lavished jewels, money and magnificent dresses upon Eugenie and built her her own palace. Her mother and grandmother had come too, Jagatjit stipulating that they would only be tolerated at the palace if they became Eugenie's maids. It was another five years before he asked Eugenie to marry him. Her mother and grandmother encouraged her to formalise the union as she would have far more security as a wife than as a mistress.

Eugenie accepted his proposal. They were married according to Sikh Anand rites in 1942 and Eugenie took the name Tara Devi. There was, however, no formal European marriage ceremony. The British came to know of the marriage and questioned the maharajah. Intelligence reports suggested the maharajah's subjects were opposed to the marriage, as were the politically active Akalis, a militant Sikh political group agitating for Sikh autonomy. The British blamed the marriage on the fact that Jagatjit and Tara Devi had been socializing with Joan and Taley Palanpur in Mussoorie. Previously the maharajah had been satisfied with having Eugenie merely as a mistress.

Princess Ourmila describes Tara Devi as having been very different from Anita. She was tall and very beautiful, with blue eyes and chestnut hair. She was shy and unwilling to mix socially. Given her lowly background, the British and the Indians viewed her with disdain, as they had Anita. Jagatjit promised the British that the marriage was a private union and that Tara Devi would only be known as 'Madame', but after a while his demands grew. First he asked that she be called 'Rani', then 'Maharani' but not 'Her Highness'. Finally he asked that she be recognized unofficially, since they moved so much together in society. The British discouraged their officials from meeting her, however, and she was not allowed to attend functions at which British officials would be present, but this ban did not extend to her mother and grandmother.

One year, when the household had all gone to stay at Mussoorie at the Chateau de Kapurthala, Pura Grosupova died under suspicious circumstances. Not long after, Nina also died. Tara Devi became profoundly disturbed. She was certain that they had both been poisoned but was not sure whether it had been carried out on the maharajah's orders or whether it had been the work of the zenana women. She lived in terror of being poisoned herself.

Jarmani Dass dismissed her fears as nerves, but others, including family, believe them to have been well founded. They suggest that Jagatjit had decided to have Eugenie murdered because he was bored with her and wanted a divorce but she was holding out for a fortune in compensation. Jagatjit had already paid a million rupees to his son's English lover Stella so he was in no mood to give in to the avarice of another European woman.

She and the maharajah were having difficulties in their marriage. Jagatjit's roving eye had alighted on a beautiful Indian girl and so Tara, too, looked elsewhere for love. She took a young lover – Major Y.B. Singh, one of her husband's officers.

Tara Devi had no friends or family to whom she could confide. Who would take her fears seriously? Certainly no one in Europe would believe that her husband had been instrumental in the deaths of her grandmother and mother. Profoundly depressed, she moved into a boarding house below the Chateau de Kapurthala. She wanted to leave India but the British refused to give her a passport. She then fled to Maiden's Hotel in Delhi, accompanied by Major Singh and her staff officers. She caught a taxi out to the Qutab Minar, a stone tower of seventy-three metres built in 1193. From the marbled fifth storey she fell three storeys to the red sandstoned second floor and her body was found hanging over the railings. Some say she had her beloved little pekes with her when she jumped, one under each arm.

Jagatjit was shocked and upset when he heard of Tara Devi's death and aged overnight. She was buried in Nicholson Cemetery near St James's Church in Delhi.

DOLLY PARNELL

married Prince Nasir Ali Khan of Rampur

Dolly Parnell was of humble origins and worked as an actress. Prince Nasir Ali Khan of Rampur first saw her in 1907 when she was appearing in 'My Darling', a musical comedy staged at London's Globe Theatre. He sent flowers to her dressing room and invited her to join him for supper. Nasir was charming and had impeccable manners. Few of Dolly's admirers treated her as respectfully as he did and as he was an Indian prince she assumed he was rich. The relationship blossomed.

Rampur, a nine-hundred-square-mile principality in the United Provinces, was ruled by Shia Muslims who had been awarded a fifteen-gun salute by the British. Nasir was the brother of the nawab of Rampur, Hamid Ali Khan. Hamid, who was the leader of the Shias of northern India, was considered the most remarkable of Rampur's rulers. He was a renowned scholar and had one of the world's finest libraries of Arabic, Persian and Urdu manuscripts. He was a gourmand of note, and had ninety to hundred cooks, each specializing in only one thing. He ate sparingly but well, having one exquisite meal a day at 7.30 p.m. He was also known for his habit of spending most of the day in the bathroom, dispensing justice and advice from a toilet seat especially designed by his chief engineer to give the impression that he was formally enthroned.

In 1894, when Nasir was eleven, Hamid had sent him to England, ostensibly for his education. Hamid was concerned that when Nasir was older he might intrigue with malcontents in the state and prove a threat to him.

Nasir was tall, dark and athletic and won many friends at Oxford University, as well as many female admirers. His tutor, one Mr Massfield, described Nasir as 'an excellent character'. In 1905 he met and fell in love with Ethel Hodkins, the daughter of a wealthy bric-a-brac and artware dealer on Bond Street. The couple became engaged. Ethel's father consented to the marriage and set Ethel's inheritance at hundred thousand pounds on the proviso that Nasir agreed to become a naturalized Englishman and renounce his claim to the throne of Rampur. The engagement eventually fell through. It was two years later that he met Dolly.

On 24 November 1909, at 12.30 p.m. in the registrar's office in Marylebone Road, London, Dolly and Nasir were married. It was a quiet wedding bereft of the pomp and circumstance of a royal wedding in India, but Nasir had done the unforgivable in his choice of marriage partner. Being orthodox Muslims, the Shia royalty of Rampur only married Shias of equal aristocratic rank. Dolly was doubly beyond the pale, being not only a Christian but also an actress.

When the press interviewed Dolly after her wedding she played down her association with the theatre, claiming only a recent and fairly superficial contact, having toured with James Welch in *When Knights Were Bold* and with George Dance's company in *The Girls of Gottenberg*. She told reporters of her Anglo-Celtic origins, saying her father came from Somerset and her mother's family from Ireland.

As a prince from a wealthy state Nasir was accustomed to a certain standard of living but his properties in Rampur were modest. In all, he owned three gardens, three houses, eleven shops and a portion of Barvala village. The couple's combined income was not enough to sustain their lavish European lifestyle, but Nasir was ill-equipped to work for his living. He had been brought up to be a gentleman of leisure. By 1912 they also had a daughter to support. Nasir appealed to his brother for money.

Just before he died, Hamid Ali Khan named his nephew Syed Raza Ali Khan as successor. Nasir railed against the injustice but there was nothing he could do. Moreover, like his uncle before him, Syed also believed that Nasir would plot against him if he returned to India, so it was impossible for Dolly and Nasir to have gone to live in Rampur even if they had wished to do so.

Destitute, Nasir asked Syed for financial support, but his nephew was not forthcoming. Syed had no interest in helping his uncle. Vicious and unpredictable, his interests lay elsewhere. The nawab had a weakness for famous prostitutes and young men and would incarcerate his young male lovers if they did the slightest thing to offend him. On hearing that one of his subjects had an exceptionally beautiful wife Syed asked the man to divorce her and hand her over. The man refused and the couple fled only to be captured by the nawab's minions and thrown into the Rampur jail. Syed had servants to cater to his every whim. He even had courtiers whose sole function was to remove the cigarettes from his mouth. If a servant or adviser displeased him he was put to death by chloroform.

Nasir, Dolly and their daughter resigned themselves to a life of relative poverty in the south of France.

ELSIE THOMPSON

married Gopal Narain Singh,
maharajah of Tikari

On 7 April 1928 *The Melbourne Truth* wrote, 'She was an Australian actress, fair of skin and form, with a bright, vivacious temperament which captivated the dark prince and made him her slave.' The actress so described was Elsie Thompson, the maharani of Tikari whose stage name was Elsie Forrest.

Elsie was born at Millers Point in Sydney on 2 August 1883. Her father, James Thompson, had emigrated from England in 1877. In 1880 in Sydney he married Balmain-born Mary Roffey. Their first child, Walter, was born in 1881, followed two years later by Elsie. James was an articulate and well read man who was 'very English' in his ways. He opened a bookshop at Erskine Street, Sydney. He became a Justice of the Peace and returning officer for the Sydney electorates of Lang and West Sydney.

James sent both his children to Fort Street High School where Elsie, with her good looks and spirited nature, excelled in dramatics and always played the glamorous role in the school play. A contemporary at school described Elsie as 'different'. Certainly she was the apple of her father's eye, and even while she was a schoolgirl men were attracted to her.

After leaving school Elsie joined a variety theatre group, calling herself Elsie Forrest. *The Truth* newspaper noted that she became 'associated' with singer and dancer Arthur Nelson at the Bijou Theatre in Melbourne in 1902. In 1903 she joined Lee and Riall's World Entertainers and left to tour South Africa. In Capetown, on 11 June 1903, she married American George Stillwell who at the time was a conjuror with the company. The two of them then joined Eugene Sandow, and in 1904 left South Africa for Calcutta.

At that time Calcutta had a rich social life and a large European population which included many Australians. Most of the Australians in Calcutta were associated with horses and horse racing. There were exporters and breeders, trainers, strappers and jockeys. Many gravitated to Woodlands, the Calcutta home of Raj Rajendra (Rajey) Narayan, the maharajah of Cooch Behar, and it was here that Elsie and Rajey met. There, in the cottage belonging to his English chauffeur Mr Davidson (the first person to drive a car in Calcutta), jockeys and the lesser lights of the racing business congregated.

Rajey Cooch Behar had an even more liberal attitude towards the West and Westerners than most Indian princes. His maternal grandfather was the great Indian liberal and religious reformer Keshub Chunder Sen. In the face of a public outcry Keshub had affianced his daughter Sunity Devi to Maharajah Nripendra Narayan Bhup Bahadur of Cooch Behar. Keshub was known for his westernized ideas, having spoken out against many Indian customs, including child marriage. He was publicly scorned for marrying his daughter at a young age to the Cooch Behar maharajah.

Sunity and Nripendra's son was born at Woodlands on 11 April 1882. His grandfather Keshub named him Raj Rajendra, king of kings, but he was nicknamed 'Rajey'.

Initially he studied at Mayo, the Princes' College. Then, in 1894, he was sent to Mr Carter's Preparatory School at Farnborough in England, becoming the first Indian prince to receive an English education. In 1897 he was accepted at Eton

Elsie Thompson and her husband, the maharajah of Tikari

and in 1900 went on to Oxford University. After his return to India, Rajey joined the Imperial Cadet Corps and finally got a commission in the Westminster Dragoons.

At the time Elsie and Rajey met, he was a heavy drinker, almost certainly an alcoholic. His mother blamed his drinking on a fall from a polo pony in Trouville, France. He was unconscious for days and when he awoke was given nothing but champagne by the doctors. This, his mother believed, was the beginning of his downfall. In any case Rajey himself took seriously a prediction made by his astrologers that he would not live beyond the age of thirty-two.

Woodlands was a white stucco building with Ionic columns flanking deep verandahs and was the third grandest residence in Calcutta, surpassed only by the Viceregal Lodge and Government House. It was a beacon of European social activity. In the grounds there were cricket pitches, a riding track and two tennis courts, and guests found plenty of amusement within its gracious, well proportioned rooms. At one time the sons of Tipu Sultan were imprisoned in the house and people believed their ghosts still haunted its rooms. The gardens were a delight, with the beds planted seasonally. There was jasmine, frangipani and roses. The red gravel drive was flanked by tall spreading trees and thickets of ornamental shrubs and bushes.

In January 1905 George Stillwell came to Sydney, ostensibly to help his father-in-law in the bookshop. Elsie was engaged to tour England but the contract fell through. According to *The Sydney Morning Herald*, in December 1905, Elsie returned to Sydney to confront her husband, who was working at the time with Thurston's Company, over his adulterous conduct with another woman. Stillwell admitted the relationship but refused to give the woman up, so in 1906 Elsie divorced him on the grounds of adultery.

It seems, however, that before Elsie had left India she had fallen in love with Rajey Cooch Behar and he had asked her to marry him. The two of them had agreed that she would return to Australia to obtain her divorce while Rajey worked on his parents to get them to agree to the marriage. Though he went into a rage and issued threats, they were adamant: he was not going to shame the family by marrying an actress.

In June 1906 Elsie cabled Rajey to let him know her divorce had gone through uncontested and that she was about to take ship for India. It is here that versions of events differ.

Colonel John Wakefield was told by his father, who managed the maharajah of Tikari's estates, that Rajey had, at this stage, become extremely ill because of his excessive drinking. Fearing imminent death and unable to fulfill his engagement promise to Elsie, he asked his best friend, Rajie Tikari, to meet her in Colombo on her return from Australia and to break the news of Rajey's terminal illness while accompanying her on a tour of India. Rajie duly met Elsie but was unable to summon up the courage to break the news that her fiancé was dying. Things became difficult, with Elsie asking at each halt, 'Will Rajey be meeting us here?' When, in due course, Tikari received news of Rajey's death, he felt sorry for Elsie and proposed to her himself.

This story is unlikely to be true, given that records show that Rajey Cooch Behar died in 1913, four years after Elsie and Tikari's marriage. (His niece Maharani Gayatri Devi of Jaipur tells that in 1911 Rajey Cooch Behar fell in love with an English actress, Edna May, but his family refused to let him marry her, as they had Elsie. He swore that if they continued to oppose his marriage he would drink himself to death. This he proceeded to do, exclusively in champagne.)

According to other sources, when Elsie cabled Rajey from Australia to tell him that her divorce had gone through, he was frantic. He knew Elsie was of a forthright nature and might make a public scene when she found out that his parents had not agreed to their marriage. He therefore persuaded his friend Rajie Tikari to meet Elsie's ship in Colombo and explain Rajey's dilemma.

In early 1907 the smooth-tongued Rajie met Elsie and escorted her to the Galle Face Hotel, haunt of the European elite whose ships dropped anchor in Ceylon. Elsie was at her charming best. Beautiful women brought out the best in Rajie. Rajie promised to show Elsie the beauty of his country, her impressions to date based upon her months in overcrowded and impoverished Calcutta.

They toured extensively. Elsie was particularly smitten with Kashmir, where the two of them stayed aboard the houseboat of Ranbir Singh of Jind. It was an idyllic period and Rajie promised to build Elsie a houseboat that would outstrip all others in terms of modern accoutrements and luxurious furnishings.

Tikari state originated, so the legend goes, with an ancestor who enjoyed success plundering the Mughal caravans plying between Delhi and Patna. The emperor realized the only way to stop the attacks was to give charge of the area to the most successful dacoit. The dacoit was gifted lands by the emperor and became the maharajah of Tikari. The Tikaris were more like zamindars than royal rulers though they were wealthier than the rulers of many salute states. They were said to be the richest landowners in Bihar.

Rajie assumed the throne through his maternal grandfather, the ruler of Tikari. The title passed on to Rajie's mother who became maharani of Tikari. She married a commoner land-owner called Babu Umbica Pershad. In 1899 when Rajie was seven, his mother died and he became maharajah. His father became guardian until Rajie attained his majority. Rajie was

educated by English tutors, Miss Joyce and Mr Keith, who
schooled him in the ways of an English gentleman. The female
rulers of Tikari who preceded Rajie had been very frugal, so
when he succeeded there was a great deal of money in the
treasury. Nevertheless, he managed to spend it all in six or
seven years.

From the time of their trip to Kashmir, Elsie and Rajie lived
as husband and wife. Rajie already had a wife. On 2 May
1909, in Lucknow, known as 'the centre of fun and frolic',
Elsie became his second wife when they married according to
the rites of the Arya Samaj. Elsie had converted to Hinduism
– the Arya Samaj, unlike orthodox Hinduism, permit converts
– and took on the name Sita Devi.

Theatrical to the tips of her toes, Elsie loved dressing up.
Her marriage was the ideal opportunity to satisfy her love of
romance. She wore the dress of a traditional Hindu bride: a
silk brocade Benares sari woven with pure gold thread. Rajie
had given her some beautiful pieces of jewellery, especially
pearls and diamonds. She wore her hair parted in the middle,
and tied in a chignon. She was especially fond of the Indian
custom of wearing armlets and she wore a pair given her by
Rajie that was studded with precious jewels.

Rajie bestowed a lifetime annuity upon Elsie that was to
be transferable to her descendants. It was a guarantee of
maintenance that carried no caveats about chaste behaviour
or remarriage.

According to John Wakefield, Rajie was not good looking
but his personality endeared him to everyone. He was funny,
a great sportsman, a first class motorist, fiercely loyal and
extremely generous. A visitor to the palace would only have
to say they wanted something and it would be in their bag
when they left. His manager would try to keep him away from
his peasants, for if they told him they were in straitened

circumstances he would suspend their revenue payments for twenty years. He would even give away land that was not his to give.

Rajie was a generous husband as well. He presented Elsie with her own Rolls Royce, provided her with unlimited overseas first-class travel and the services of her own Parisian hairdresser. He gave her many wonderful jewels, including a diamond necklace worth eighty to ninety lakh rupees. These were the diamonds described by *The Melbourne Truth* when Elsie visited Sydney in the summer of 1917:

> ... she attended a patriotic ball in the Town Hall. The gorgeousness of her dress and the richness of her jewels made men gasp and women envious. She was reputed to have worn 75,000 pounds worth of diamonds.

Rajie's main residence, the White House, was located in Gaya, a place of pilgrimage where devout Hindus flocked seeking to breathe their last on the river Falgu's holy banks. Gaya was not to Elsie's liking. Not only was it small and parochial, it was also dusty and hot. (Later, Rajie's Muslim wife Sayeeda Khatoon would describe it as a place where the river had no water, the land no mountains and the men no brains.)

Elsie hated living in Gaya and most of all she hated the White House's proximity to the Red House, occupied by the Wakefields. J.G. Wakefield, Tikari's estate manager and patriarch of the family, was Rajie's closest friend. The two men had been at school together at St George's in Mussoorie, and had met again when Rajie had been in Mussoorie on holiday. At that time 'J.G.' was an engineer on the railways. When Rajie fell ill with cholera and his servants fled in terror, J.G. remained

Sita Devi (Elsie Thompson)

with him and nursed him back to health. Rajie invited him to return with him to Tikari to serve as his secretary. No two friends could have been closer. (In fact they died within a month of each other. When J.G. died it was said that Rajie promptly willed himself to death.) J.G.'s four children grew up side by side with Rajie's children. Elsie was fiercely jealous of J.G.'s influence over Rajie and did her best to undermine the friendship. In turn J.G. viewed her as a cheap opportunist who had married Rajie for his money.

Patna was no more to Elsie's liking. The Sultanganj Palace, Rajie's palace on the banks of the Ganges, was the principal residence of Rajie's first wife, Maharani Vijayawada. Patna, later to become the capital of Bihar, was simply a larger version of Gaya.

In Tikari town, the original parcel of land given to the Tikaris by the Mughals was Killa Fort, massive and sprawling, spreading out far beyond the perimeters of Tikari town proper. Killa had been given to Maharani Vijayawada on her marriage to Rajie and its caretakers would remain faithful to her even after her death. Tikari town was served by schools and a hospital and the land around abounded in mustard seed and was cooled by huge mango trees dripping with fruit. The legend that a treasure was buried under the overmantel in the zenana of Killa Fort gave it a fairy-tale quality. But it was far too small and isolated to ever appeal to Elsie as a full-time residence.

Elsie's favourite home was Rajie's hunting lodge at Balwa, set amidst dense jungle teeming with elephants, tigers, deer and bears. From the house to the front gate fifteen rose bushes had been planted and were kept moistened by water pumped up from the Falgu River flowing less than a hundred metres from the house. Rajie had fitted Balwa with all the latest modern amenities so that the comforts of the city could be enjoyed in a unique and beautiful setting.

Elsie Thompson

Rajie had a portrait painted of Elsie dressed in a dark blue silk sari with two Great Danes standing sentinel. It stood above the mantelpiece in direct line of vision as guests entered the building via the porte-cochere. They were left in no doubt as to who the chatelaine of Balwa Hunting Lodge was.

Rajie's hospitality was legendary, especially to the British, and he and Elsie entertained on a grand scale at Balwa. John Wakefield tells of a partridge shoot the maharajah laid on for the governor of Bihar. Though there were no partridges in that part of Bihar, the maharajah felt it incumbent on him as a good host to obtain enough partridges to provide a satisfactory shoot. Wakefield tells how the bird markets of Calcutta and Lucknow were scoured for three months for partridges and how they

> ... came in huge crates and the old station was nothing but partridges for about a month. There must have been at least five thousand of them, all calling away 'Kain, Kain' for all they were worth.

Apart from Balwa it was Calcutta where Elsie spent most of her married life. There she showed her dogs, taking many first prizes at the Calcutta Dog Show. But it was the horse races and the social life associated with them which appealed to her most of all. Much of the racing scene during Elsie's time was dominated by Australians. Australian breeders and exporters formed a strong contingent in the city; many brought their wives and daughters with them. Elsie still had her contacts from her days in Calcutta when she had become engaged to Rajey Cooch Behar.

Calcutta's *Empress* magazine commented upon Elsie's popularity in this cosmopolitan city. Alice Murray Smith, daughter of Australian Steve Margrett, who had a substantial interest in the Calcutta horse trade, recalled 'the absolutely marvellous social life'. There were polo carnivals, steeplechase meets, weekly race events; there were the clubs, the restaurants like Firpos; there were parties and the regular parade along Red Road to the music of the viceroy's band.

A description of the Viceroy's Cup in the early twentieth century (it and the Governor's Cup being the two most important polo carnivals) gives some idea of its popularity:

> ... 100,000 brightly dressed people in the centre of the course when the Viceroy and his party arrived ... three carriages with six horses in each and ridden by postillions and with his wonderful troop of Bodyguard, 300 beautiful well trained horses before the carriages and 300 behind. These were all big bay horses over 16 hands high, and beautifully turned out, each horse was ridden by a native over six feet who was dressed in blue uniform with a red and blue turban and red and blue sash, and each man carrying a red and blue pennant. When the whole troop came up the straight between thousands of cheering and brightly dressed natives, it was truly a wonderful sight.

December 1 to the end of February was the height of Calcutta's sport and social season and Elsie made sure she didn't miss a minute of the excitement.

Elsie and Rajie participated in many major social events, such as the 1911 Delhi Durbar at which King George V and Queen Mary presided. Rajie had a major role in the proceedings and though Elsie could not appear at official functions as the maharani of Tikari she still took part in numerous unofficial activities.

As soon as the First World War began Rajie took a loan from the maharajah of Dharbanga and donated a squadron of tanks to the war effort. He travelled to Europe to enlist and became a lieutenant despatch rider to Field Marshal Haig. While he was away Elsie continued with her hectic social life in Calcutta and in Australia.

Rajie was an inveterate womanizer and in time he and Elsie began to find their amusement separately. While Elsie did not approve, she was in no position to complain given that she herself had not been circumspect. They managed to retain the form of their marriage, however, by heeding some ground rules.

With love gone, Rajie grew increasingly irritated by Elsie's bossiness and outspokenness. He complained to J.G. that Elsie had 'gotten too big for her boots'. Rajie found himself having to ask her permission to use the Rolls. Then when he wanted to have his hair cut by Elsie's Parisian hairdresser, he was told he had to get the maharani's permission. Rajie was furious. He now realized it was his money that Elsie had married. How was he to divest himself of a wife without losing a fortune? Elsie was no meek Indian wife who would accept divorce without a sizeable settlement. He had already settled an annuity on her which was legally binding. He consulted J.G. who told him to talk to his legal advisor Sir Sultan Ahmad. Then he hit on a solution. If he could prove they had not been legally married in the first place it would absolve him of any financial responsibility. He knew that George Stillwell and Elsie had colluded in getting a divorce.

In the meantime Elsie had met and fallen for Ernest Ivan Jones, a wealthy Australian horse exporter with substantial financial interests in India as well as in Melbourne and in Perth. Ernest was a larger-than-life figure – 'a man's man'. He was equally taken by Elsie, despite the fact that at thirty-eight she was no longer the beauty she had once been.

Ernest swept Elsie off her feet. It was easy for them to spend time together in Calcutta without arousing suspicion. The two of them were both regulars at all the horse events.

Even though they were discreet, Rajie came to know of the liaison. The relationship suited his interests because his Muslim courtesan, Sayeeda Khatoon, was pressing him for marriage. Sayeeda now had two sons and a daughter. She wanted to regularize the union so that she and her children could enjoy some official status. Now he had two cards he could play in his battle to be rid of Elsie: a potentially illegal marriage and adultery.

At the White House, Elsie and Rajie had a huge argument. They stormed and screamed and Rajie told Elsie to get out. She asked for the Rolls to take her to Gaya railway station but Rajie now had his moment of triumph. He refused, screaming, 'Go by tum-tum [horse drawn cart].' Rajie was immovable. Desperate, she fled in tears to her old foe in the Red House, J.G., and begged him to intercede. J.G. arranged for her to be lodged in the dak bungalow while he arranged for transport to Calcutta. Elsie was not unhappy with the prospect of being with Ernest but was furious about the way Rajie had treated her.

Elsie found refuge with Ernest in Calcutta and when Rajie heard they were living together he stopped Elsie's annuity. There were calls enough on his money from Sayeeda Khatoon, who by now had produced two more sons, and her family was taking advantage of Rajie's legendary generosity. It was now 1921 and Elsie was living the high life and was not interested in the politics of Tikari. Nor was she much interested in her annuity. Ernest had more than enough to satisfy her every whim. Besides, she hadn't left Tikari empty-handed. She had taken her jewellery, which made even the wives of Calcutta's richest nawabs gasp with admiration.

In 1923 Rajie went to court to have his marriage to Elsie declared invalid. He claimed that he was not obliged to abide by the terms of their marriage agreement and pay Elsie her allowance as she had deceived him by not being divorced from her first husband when they married. He argued that her divorce from Stillwell was fraudulent and obtained through collusion. Rajie succeeded in his claim and the marriage was declared invalid. But Elsie, furious, countersued. The high court then ruled that the marriage was binding and that Elsie was entitled to her annuity.

The Australian press picked up the story. In 1928 *The Melbourne Truth* wrote: 'Her Dark Prince ... Elsie Forrest's Very Own Maharajah ... He Stopped Her Allowance.' Every Australian paper wanted a statement from Elsie but as she was busy in Calcutta prosecuting her case, the press made up their own stories. *The Truth* wrote of 'Eastern rulers who have frequently tried to secure Australian girls for their harems' and of poor Elsie who 'as a Hindu woman became an abject slave'. The Elsie who graced the racetracks and clubs of Calcutta was not the Elsie they created. *The Truth* wrote,

> As the favourite wife of the Maharajah she might wear richly beautiful Parisian clothes and gems that cost a fortune; but such ornamentation was only for her husband's eyes, for though the native rulers and princes of India entertain on a grand scale, at such functions none of their own women is allowed to be present.

Having lost his case in the high court Rajie decided to take it to the Privy Council. On 30 November 1931, the Privy Council ruled in Elsie's favour. She had a right to her annuity along with interest, backdated to 1921 when it had been stopped. If Elsie decided to take up the award, Rajie confided to friends, the state of Tikari would be brought to its knees.

But Elsie's attention was with Ernest and their life in Melbourne. None of his family approved of Elsie and there was some friction. His wife, Marie, from whom he was separated, lived in Sydney. One of his sons, Owen, lived in Carnarvon in Western Australia and his other son, Jack, lived in Perth. In 1932 Ernest had bought Mundrabilla Station, a half-million-acre property on the southern edge of the Nullarbor Plains in Western Australia. He intended to settle his sons on the property to run sheep and breed horses. It was on a visit to Perth late that year that he had a heart attack and died.

Elsie was devastated. He had supported her in grand style for the ten years since she had left Rajie. She put her own notice in the West Australian papers titled 'What a Man'.

Ernest left an estate in Melbourne valued at fifty-one thousand pounds. The probate notice in the *Argus* stated that after legacies to friends and provision for his sister the estate was left in trust for his family. The will stipulated that not only should Elsie occupy the house he owned in Fordholm Road, Melbourne and freely enjoy its lavish contents, but she was also to have the income from the investment of 22,500 pounds for the rest of her life.

Elsie had befriended a woman named Myrtle Mcleod, who worked for a Melbourne jeweller and used to clean her pearls. She asked Myrtle if she would come and live with her and be her companion. Myrtle agreed and moved in. The two women got on famously, Elsie regaling Myrtle with her stories of India. But Myrtle was disturbed by Elsie's so-called friends from the Toorak area who began hanging about and 'borrowing' Elsie's splendid jewels, most of which were never returned. She was also concerned about Elsie's heavy drinking.

Elsie took a break from Melbourne, trying to shake off the social parasites that saw her as an easy target. She stayed with friends Emma and Joe Binstead in Manly in Sydney. She did not bother to contact her brother Walter who thoroughly disapproved of her and thought her loud, vulgar and immoral. Her father, who had talked incessantly of 'the rich Maharanee who would help him see England again', had died in 1930. Elsie had been in Melbourne at the time and had been too caught up in her own life to attend his funeral.

From Manly, Elsie wrote to an old friend of Rajie's in Gaya to ask him to intervene with Rajie about her money. Rajie wrote back saying he thought they should 'let bygones be bygones' and 'bury the hatchet'. He agreed to Elsie's suggestion that they meet and sort out their differences over money and closed by asking her to let him know how much he should send her.

Elsie wrote to him again and again, but no money eventuated. At the end of 1934, Willie Hathaway, Rajie's new manager who had taken over from J.G. Wakefield, wrote to Elsie at Rajie's behest explaining that numerous court cases had prevented Rajie from meeting up with her, as he had suggested the year before, in New Zealand. Elsie scathingly annotated the letter with the fact that Willie had formerly been a draper in Mussoorie.

By this time Elsie was being pressured to leave the Fordholm Road house. Mundrabilla had been sold and Ernst's family was keen to see his assets liquidated. In 1936, in desperation, Elsie wrote to her lawyer in London, S.L. Polak, asking him for his assistance. In Allahabad Polak met with Sir Sultan Ahmed, Rajie's legal adviser, to try to work out a compromise on Elsie's behalf. Ahmed said if Elsie wrote to him outlining the facts as well as her demands he would place it before Rajie.

Elsie had gradually isolated herself from all her old friends and her family had not seen her for years. In 1939, Leah, an old stage friend who had been one of her best friends in the Calcutta days, wrote to her asking, 'What have I done to you that you have so definitely stopped writing to me?' But Leah was not alone. Apart from people who might put her case forward with Rajie, Elsie had turned her back on her Indian life.

Myrtle McLeod stayed with Elsie until Myrtle's mother became ill and she had to return home to nurse her. When Myrtle visited the Fordholm Road house she found Elsie was drinking more heavily than ever. In January 1949 Elsie was arrested by the police and taken to the Royal Park Hospital. It seems someone had phoned the police complaining about Elsie's boisterous behaviour. At the Royal Park Elsie was diagnosed as suffering from manic depressive insanity. No one, it seemed, believed her stories. Who but a maniac would talk about stables full of royal elephants, forts filled with treasure and a princely husband who was as rich as Croesus?

So they committed the mad maharani, writing on her file 'suffers grandiose delusions'. But Elsie was sane enough to convince them she was English rather than Australian and that she had been born in 1889 – her vanity insisting she was six years younger than she really was. The admissions staff entered her vocation as 'opera actress', and 'singer' as her occupation before retirement. They noted she had solitary habits and was tearful. She admitted she had spells of depression, which was hardly surprising. With Ernest gone, Elsie had lost her lover, her admirer and her protector.

Myrtle was distraught when she found out about Elsie's committal. Later she wrote to her friend Elsie Kunz 'that Elsie was never a mental case'. Myrtle told those who would listen that there had been a dire purpose behind Elsie's forcible interment. Elsie Kunz noted in the family history that Ernest's 'family made her life difficult' and 'those who had reason to do so saw to it that she was committed to Royal Park Mental Hospital'.

In March 1949, Elsie was transferred to the Sunbury Mental Hospital. Their report notes she was garrulous and hypomanic and showed signs of deterioration and memory impairment. She was allowed out in December 1949 but three months later she was readmitted as she was unable to manage for herself without Myrtle's assistance. In 1962 Elsie was transferred to the Kew Mental Hospital. She was discharged on 1 September 1964 but it was only twenty-four days before she was readmitted.

All the while Myrtle kept visiting her old friend. Myrtle had finally moved into a tiny housing commission flat. She managed to find a nursing home for Elsie and used to visit her every day, taking her washing home and bringing her tasty tidbits. The matron asked Myrtle if she could keep Elsie for a few weeks until a single room became vacant as Elsie was getting a little too boisterous for the other patients. But Myrtle was unable to do this, fearing that if the housing commission discovered that she had someone living with her they might ask her to give up the flat.

So Elsie was sent back to Kew. Myrtle continued to visit, taking coffee, chicken sandwiches and fruit. For her birthday, Myrtle asked Elsie what she would like. Elsie said she would like some curried prawns 'like I showed you we did in India'. 'So you see she never forgot,' Myrtle wrote to Elsie Kunz. It seems that Elsie had also remembered the 'borrowed' jewellery and was mourning its loss.

Elsie began losing weight and by November 1967 she was just skin and bone. She was diagnosed with cancer and on the evening of 21 November the matron rang Myrtle to tell her that Elsie was sinking fast. Myrtle arrived by bus at 6 a.m. but Elsie had died in the early hours of the morning. The authorities had earlier tried, without success, to contact Elsie's brother.

Elsie's ashes were interred at the Cheltenham Lawn Cemetery. Apart from Myrtle there were no mourners. Myrtle asked if Elsie could be cremated with 'a nice rose tree over her ashes', but the authorities said she would have to pay for it and Myrtle was penniless. The tiny amount that she had saved from her pension had been spent on the little luxuries she had brought Elsie.

The funeral directors were paid by the Public Trustee of Victoria for no relatives could be found. Unrecognized for the final twenty years of her life, she was also forgotten in death. She lay in an unmarked grave for six years until her niece was tracked down, who then had a plaque engraved with the words Sita Devi, Maharani of Tikari.

Rajie had died of a heart attack in Gaya in 1958, within a month of the death of his old friend J.G. There had been a great skirmish over his body. The Hindu priests feared that his Muslim family would attempt to take the body away and bury it, which was anathema to them, so they stole it and he was cremated at the Vishnupat Temple on the banks of the Falgu River. By this time, Elsie was in the Sunbury Mental Hospital. It is unlikely she ever knew about Rajie's death.

MOLLY FINK

married Martanda Bhairava Tondaiman,
rajah of Pudukkottai

*E*sme Mary 'Molly' Sorrett Fink was born in Melbourne, Australia on 15 September 1894. She was the second daughter of barrister Wolfe Fink and his wife Elizabeth. Wolfe Fink was a refined man, an intellectual, but he was not good at managing money.

Wolfe rented a series of houses in Melbourne including Aorangi, a solid two-storey Victorian residence where Molly was born. Though asset-poor, Wolfe made sure his family were experience-rich and that there was always enough money for his childrens' education at the best of schools. Molly, along with her sister Ida and young brother Ossie, was enrolled at Lauriston School. Here Molly studied English, German, French and Latin, but she was remembered by her classmates principally for her high spirits and her knowingness about the opposite sex.

Molly left Lauriston at fifteen, 'under a cloud', perhaps for misbehaviour. This abrupt end to her schooldays did not affect her unduly. Her great love at the time was theatre-going, and she especially enjoyed musical comedy. Just before the First World War the Fink family toured the Dutch East Indies but on their return tragedy struck, with Wolfe suddenly dying of a ruptured aorta.

His death left the family almost penniless. Elizabeth scraped together enough money to rent an apartment in the elegant

Hotel Majestic Mansions which had a large turnover of upper-class patrons. Elizabeth had made the choice with an eye to finding her girls rich husbands who would rescue them from poverty.

Martanda Bhairava Tondaiman was born on 26 November 1875. He was the third son of Rajah Ramachandra Tondaiman's eldest daughter, but was formally adopted by his grandfather who had no male heir. Martanda was installed on the gaddi on 2 May 1886 and attained his majority and full ruling powers in 1894.

Martanda showed early promise under his Cambridge-educated tutor Fredric Feilden Crossley, being a diligent student. He was also good at sports. It was inevitable, given that his education had instilled in him an admiration of all things European, that Martanda wanted to travel to Europe and spend time in European company. The British official community in Pudukkottai and Trichinopoly was too small to keep him amused. He wanted to visit the art galleries, museums, and great country houses with the splendid shooting they offered. He wanted to spend time in Europe's health resorts and he wanted to socialise with beautiful, sophisticated European women. He complained that no woman of his own lowly Kallar caste was sufficiently educated to interest him.

Pudukkottai, which covered twelve hundred square miles and had an eleven-gun salute, was a small state by the standards of princely India. Its revenue was insufficient to sustain Martanda in the lavish style he favoured and still leave a surplus for public works or charitable endowments. As an example of his outgoings, Martanda employed 924 servants at his Trichinopoly palace, whereas the nawab of Palanpur had a staff of 125 in his similarly-sized Zora Mahal palace. Martanda also owned the old palace in Pudukkottai and had embarked on building a new palace. By the time it was finished in 1924, however, he had left India for good. In the hill station of Kodaikanal he owned two cottages, and he also possessed entire villages in and around Pudukkottai. (In time, one of the Kodaikanal cottages became home to Molly's brother-in-law, 'Uncle Do', and his Scottish wife Muriel Briggs.)

Martanda had for some years been warned by the British authorities against making an alliance with a European woman. He had had affairs with white women and had at one time been engaged to an American. The authorities feared that his next step would be marriage.

In March 1915 Martanda came to Australia on a visit, his arrival preceded by a cabled request from the governor-general of India that the rajah's entry not be impeded. This was the heyday of the 'White Australia' policy and there was the possibility that Australian customs officials might otherwise require the rajah to undergo the humiliation of being required to take a dictation test.

In Sydney Martanda became a frequent visitor to the races at Royal Randwick and was warmly welcomed at numerous parties by Sydney's social elite. They poked fun at his dress sense and his name, while he was polite and convivial and probably somewhat bored. That is until he met Molly Fink in the dining room of the Australia Hotel.

Molly and her sister Ida, accompanied by their mother, had come on a visit from Melbourne with an eye to meeting some of Sydney's eligible bachelors. When they mentioned to Martanda that they were moving to the Hydro Majestic, a fashionable hotel in the Blue Mountains not far from Sydney, he amended his travel plans in order to join them. The group enjoyed being together and Martanda put his car and chauffeur at the Finks' disposal. When, in due course, they returned to Melbourne, Martanda followed.

Wedding portrait of Molly Fink and the rajah of Pudukkottai

On 6 April Martanda wrote to his friend Lord Pentland, the governor of Madras, telling him of the warm hospitality he had received in Australia and hinting that he had found the woman of his dreams. He had waited long enough — he was turning forty that year. Lord Pentland replied promptly, reminding Martanda of the viceroy's admonition that he marry a Hindu. Ignoring his friend's advice, Martanda went ahead and proposed to Molly. By this time they had known each other for five months.

The engagement was announced on 6 August 1915, but the news was not received in the way Molly had hoped. While her mother and sister approved of the match, the rest of her family were aghast. Her Uncle Theodore, however, hid his dismay and provided five hundred pounds for her trousseau. Official disapproval was immediately apparent, with the Australian governor-general, Sir Ronald Munro-Ferguson, refusing to attend the wedding breakfast.

With arrangements already made for a voyage to the US within a fortnight, Molly and Martanda's engagement was brief. The marriage took place on 10 August at Melbourne's registrar-general's office. Molly was a Catholic, but a Hindu groom made a church wedding out of the question.

Molly wore white taffeta and a small black hat. She carried a posy of rare green orchids, displaying a distinctive touch that would later make her one of the most stylish women of her generation. She was given away by her Uncle Theodore, watched by her mother dressed in black silk befitting her widowhood.

The ceremony was followed by luncheon at the Menzies Hotel. As a wedding gift, Martanda presented Molly with four thousand pounds worth of jewellery. Friends were to cattily observe that the diamonds hardly compensated for the disgrace of being married to a black man.

Political repercussions were immediate. On receiving a telegram from the rajah announcing his marriage, King George V wrote a furious letter to Viceroy Lord Hardinge, expressing his opposition. In turn the viceroy scathingly remarked, 'Miss Molly Fink! What a name!' From the start, official disapproval destroyed all hopes of a social life either in Australia or India that a couple of their rank could reasonably expect.

Sir Ronald Munro-Ferguson enquired of the viceroy as to whether there were 'harem or other complications' awaiting Molly in India. The Australian press and Molly's friends mused over the bizarre possibility that on her arrival in India she might have to go into purdah and be locked away from male eyes. Just ten days after Molly's wedding the *Bulletin* newspaper described Molly and her sister Ida in language redolent of the harem. They were

> ... two big-eyed darlings with oval, ivory-skinned
> faces and pouting pomegranate lips. They looked as
> if they should be dressed in Persian "bags" and veils.

On 28 August, Molly and Martanda left Sydney aboard the *Sonoma*, accompanied by Molly's mother and sister. Molly travelled with thirty-six pieces of luggage plus a maid. Their destination was San Francisco, in order to see the Panama Exhibition – a lavish celebration of the completing of the Panama Canal that covered almost eight square kilometres. In October they returned to Sydney, and in November Martanda, Molly and her mother departed for the Medina en route to Pudukkottai.

On 22 November the rajah's subjects saw his foreign bride for the first time. Molly and Martanda were greeted by a dazzling reception as their car arrived in the capital. Subramaniya Iyyer recalls the spectacle:

I was just a boy, twelve or thirteen. It was a grand procession. It started from the Brihadambal Temple and went along all the four main streets of Pudukota and they travelled in His Highness' Rolls Royce. All along the streets bamboo posts were erected. In those days there was no electric light, only lanterns, coloured lights were lit in the main streets. I saw His Highness; Molly Fink, she was a charming girl.

Molly was greeted at the palace by the women who paid homage to their new rani. Then followed entertainment provided by the palace nautch girls. The couple then emerged once more to show themselves to the rajah's subjects. Molly and Martanda travelled the streets in the state landau, drawn by four horses decked in silver and gold. They were followed by retainers carrying massive swords. It was a fairy-tale setting: jewelled elephants dressed in silver and gold lumbered through the seething mass of humanity. Cavalry in green and infantry in scarlet marched beside the landau and the elephants. People joyfully threw armfuls of perfumed flowers. The celebrations were followed by temple honours.

Martanda was optimistic about the future. He wanted to make a fresh start. His people had, he believed, welcomed his foreign wife enthusiastically, and because of this he hoped the British would officially recognize her. In the end, however, he and Molly stayed in Pudukkottai barely five months. British recognition was not forthcoming, which precluded any satisfactory social life for them and made Molly's position untenable. The political agent had informed them that if Lord Pentland, the governor of Madras, were to visit the state, only Martanda would be invited to social functions. In that case, Martanda replied, he would prefer to receive no invitations at all.

An evocative picture of the rani of Pudukkottai and her young son Martanda Sydney, circa 1917

There was also another reason for the couple leaving Pudukkottai. Soon after they arrived, Molly discovered that she was pregnant. Before long she was assailed by severe attacks of vomiting and diarrhoea. At first it was thought she was suffering from morning sickness or simply the effects of her imprudent consumption of cherries, chocolates and champagne in a hot climate. Martanda moved her to his palace at Trichinopoly but she became ill once more. Martanda then decided that a cooler climate might help. They travelled up to Ootacamund and checked into Sylks' Hotel. It was from here that a sample of Molly's vomitus was sent to Major Robb, the government medical examiner. He discovered traces of oleander — a poison used by Indians to bring on miscarriage and even death. Martanda was distraught at the news. The rajah asked the Madras government for permission to buy a house in Ootacamund. Martanda planned to staff it with handpicked people and cocoon Molly there until her confinement. But the government refused, saying that Molly's presence would be an embarrassment to Ooty's European population. So, with the shipping lanes to Europe closed because of the war, Molly and Martanda had no choice but to return to Australia.

The couple rented a harbourside mansion in Sydney, St Mervyns, where, on 22 July 1916 their son Martanda Sydney Tondaiman, Rajkumar of Pudukkottai, was born. The baby was not baptised — a sign that he was not to be raised a Christian, which would only have strengthened the case against his succession. In fact, the prince was never even to visit Pudukkottai, let alone rule it. And from that time on, his father made only the occasional, brief trip back to his state. Martanda chose to remain away from India as long as the British refused to accord Molly the titles and honours due to the wife of a rajah.

Rajah Martanda

In Sydney Martanda's main occupation was owning race horses. By degrees he and Molly came to have a wide social circle. The gossip columnists marvelled at Molly's wardrobe and jewels. The clothes she wore at Melba's farewell concert in January 1919, and at the Peace Ball (Sydney's first public ball after the war), they described in intricate detail. Before the war ended, Molly was asked to run a stall at a fete at Ascham School to raise funds for the 20th Battalion's Comfort Fund. The *Bulletin* observed that she asked record prices and got them because most of the buyers eagerly 'paid to look at her magnificent diamond and emerald earrings, her rope of pearls, and her diamond dagger brooch.'

Today in Pudukkottai some of the rajah's descendants suggest that the emeralds in Molly's jewel collection had been obtained (along with many other gems belonging to the Pudukkottai royal family) when Molly visited Pudukkottai in 1915. The Pudukkottai emeralds were legendary. According to members of the royal family, they disappeared during Rajah Martanda's reign, along with the state throne of solid gold.

In 1921, the *Times* of London reported a jewel theft that took place in the rajah's Park Lane flat in which a large six-sided emerald ring set in platinum surrounded by diamonds, a circular diamond-bordered plaque with a ruby in the centre and a diamond loop, were stolen. The Rajkumar of Pudukkottai, brother to Martanda's successor, tells of a visit to Martanda in London where he glimpsed on the side table a cigarette box whose lid was studded with an emerald the size of a large marble.

In August 1919 the Tondaimans left Australia, never to return. Martanda made a brief visit to India, in the hope of achieving official recognition for Molly, while she and their son continued on to Britain. Molly had just turned twenty-five. In November Martanda joined his wife in London, where

Martanda and Molly at their presentation to King George V

they leased an apartment in Park Lane. In June 1920 the two of them were allowed a private audience with King George V, then at the end of the year the rajah received a letter from the secretary of state for India informing him that his son was not going to be granted recognition by the British. Martanda, thoroughly disheartened, made another short visit to India in an attempt to negotiate a solution to the impasse, and eventually agreed to remain the rajah of Pudukkottai in name only, with his brother Raghunatha taking over as regent. This, the British felt, would provide stability within the state. Martanda was to receive an annual allowance plus a large lump sum from the state in compensation. He apparently felt no guilt at the enormous amount of money that the British allowed him to drain from the state's coffers.

Now freed from all his state responsibilities, Martanda returned to Europe and in 1922 he and Molly settled in Cannes. Here they bought a grand villa called La Favorite. The two-storey house had a covered semi-circular portico and was set on a large balustraded terrace. C. Milliet-Mondon, author of a monograph on Cannes villas, described La Favorite as a 'very fine example of a late nineteenth century bourgeois home' with 'beautiful proportions, sobriety and harmony'. Martanda and Molly made friends among the many British residents in the town, and Martanda once again devoted himself to his passion for horseracing. Race meetings at Longchamps, Deauville, Ascot and Epsom took up much of Molly and Martanda's time, and they were frequent visitors to London and Paris.

In social terms, Molly made a success of life abroad. She became the intimate of the duke and duchess of Kent, Elsa Maxwell, Cecil and Nancy Beaton, Lord Donegall, Lady Houston and writer William Locke. She patronized the finest couturiers of the day — Paquin, Patou, Schiaparelli, Molyneux,

Molly and Martanda at the Melbourne races

Chanel and Lanvin. Her flair as a party organizer par excellence was admired by Cannes' other rich and titled residents: 'the press descriptions of her speedboat and her glittering parties leave little doubt of her mad extravagance.'

Though Molly had given away many of her saris to her great friend Grace Tivendale on her departure from Australia in 1919, she kept some of the most exquisite pieces. When she wore them they literally took people's breath away. When Kapurthala state minister Diwan Jarmani Dass recalled his friendship with Molly and Martanda he spoke of 'often seeing them at society gatherings in London and Paris and elsewhere' and on a few occasions Molly 'wore the Indian sari in which she looked like an Indian Maharani'.

The press described an elegant dinner party hosted by Martanda and Molly in the Belgian port of Oostende, which proved spectacularly unsuccessful. Martanda had left the menu to the management of the restaurant, and they, failing to consider Martanda's Hindu sensibilities, had served a large joint of pork. Outraged and revolted, the normally gentle Martanda grabbed the dish and 'hurled the unwelcome flesh' through the window. A few minutes later, an elderly, grease-spattered priest appeared before him with an obvious complaint. An embarrassed Martanda apologized sincerely, then handed him five hundred pounds for the poor of his parish.

In the winter of 1927 Molly and Martanda leased a house in London. In the following May, they left Britain for France, probably on their way back to Cannes. In Paris, however, the rajah experienced acute intestinal pain and was taken to the new American Hospital in Neuilly. Here he underwent two emergency operations, but his condition deteriorated further and on 28 May, with Molly and his son at his bedside, he died. He was fifty-three.

As a Hindu and a ruling prince of an Indian state, Martanda's body should have been returned to Pudukkottai for cremation. Martanda had continued to be the tutelary deity of the Brihadambal Temple and the ruler of Pudukkottai state. Only with the rituals of death and cremation could the rajah's subjects properly express their grief. From Paris Molly cabled Pudukkottai officials to prepare for his cremation, but the India Office stepped in and refused to allow Martanda's body to be returned to the place of his birth.

Molly begged Lord Birkenhead and the governor of Madras to permit Martanda's body to be flown to India. A cold 'no' greeted her entreaties. They did not have the courage to tell her that if the body should be returned for cremation, and she and her son were present, they feared a upsurge of sympathy from the Pudukkottai people for her young son's right to rule. Officials at the India Office gloated as the extent of Martanda's folly in marrying a white woman became fully apparent.

Molly had to have the rajah's body embalmed and shipped to London where it was cremated at the Golders Green Crematorium according to Hindu rites. There were no subjects to watch the young Martanda, dressed in white, circle his father's coffin, or to hear the priests intone the funeral prayers, or watch as Maharajah Jagatjit Singh of Kapurthala scattered rice upon his friend's coffin. This was the point at which Martanda's line of ruling Tondaimans came to an end.

As a mark of respect, Molly wore the white of a Hindu widow for a year. Her socialite friends were impressed by her piety although it did not take long for the Aga Khan to turn up on her doorstep begging for her hand in marriage. Though Molly declined the Aga Khan, he was not to be the last in a string of male admirers who would pursue her into middle age. Donald Hamilton, marquess of Donegall, became a significant figure in her life, and she and Cecil Beaton were friends. Like other wealthy women of her time, she patronized the jewellers Cartier and Van Cleef and Arpels. She was photographed by Cecil Beaton wearing Cartier ear pendants of pearls and diamonds. After she died, her son gave the pendants to Farah Diba, the empress of Iran.

Prince Martanda Sydney was sent to Le Rosey School in Switzerland where he was desperately unhappy and utterly friendless save for the equally lonely Mohammad Reza Pahlavi, the shah of Iran – their friendship would endure for life. In 1935 Martanda was admitted into Clare College, Cambridge to study history.

Following her year of mourning, Molly returned to her hectic social life. Money slipped through her fingers like water. Osbert Lancaster described Molly in *With an Eye to the Future* as watching

> her teenage son and with gilded toe-nail and made
> up to the nines, feeding asparagus tips to a pet
> tortoise with a diamond encrusted shell.

La Favorite was sold not long after Martanda died and the proceeds divided between Molly and her son. Molly set up residence in a flat in London's Mayfair. In 1938, almost ten years to the day of the death of his father, Martanda Sydney's life was changed for ever. The prince was travelling in Molly's car, which was being driven by her chauffeur, between Cannes and Paris. They had a horrific accident and the chauffeur and Molly's maid, who was also a passenger, were killed. The prince was seriously injured. He eventually pulled through but was left with a pronounced limp that troubled him for the rest of his life.

Just before the accident, a match had been arranged for him with the daughter of one of Molly's friends. But he told his

Molly Fink, photographed by Cecil Beaton

friend Carola Koch Morton that he did not want to foist his disfigured body on a perfectly formed young wife. Eventually he did marry but the marriage proved a disaster. His wife was rowdy and an alcoholic and in drunken moments would jump onto the table and perform wild dances. Molly was horrified and Martanda was not too devastated when she ran off with another man.

Though Martanda blamed his wife's intemperate habits for the breakdown of their marriage, it was probably his homosexuality that was the deciding factor. Even if he had been heterosexual, it is unlikely that Martanda would ever have found a woman to measure up to Molly. In his eyes she was more than his mother – she was his idol and role model – and it may well have been the nature of his relationship with her that complicated his sexuality.

While in the those days it was perfectly acceptable for a woman of Molly's status and financial position to spend her life partying and looking beautiful, it was inappropriate behaviour for a man for whom the money had begun to run out. In 1945 Martanda was arrested in New York for a series of robberies that he had perpetrated on his rich friends, resulting in a humiliating public scandal. *The New York Times* reported him as having said, on being questioned, that he had 'only a couple of thousand dollars in the bank, not nearly enough to maintain my usual scale of living.' Since boyhood, Martanda had been a kleptomaniac. In his youth Molly had managed to replace what her son had stolen but by the 1940s her annuity was barely sufficient to support her own lavish lifestyle. Molly decided to leave her son to deal with the results of his actions.

Martanda was convicted and imprisoned in Sing Sing. After ten months he was deported to Cuba although the legalities of such an action were questionable given the fact he was an

American citizen. The FBI had amassed a substantial file on the prince and Molly, in his case noting his pro-Vichy and pro-Petain sympathies, and his unsurprising Anglophobia. For a while Molly's fundraising activities for the Allied war effort had raised FBI suspicions that she was using the funds for her own use, but investigations eventually showed the allegations to be untrue.

The British kept a close eye on the prince even though he had moved out of their orbit with dispossession of the Pudukkottai patrimony. His criminal activities reinforced their contention that the products of mixed race unions exemplified the worst characteristics of both. In 1946 when the nawab of Palanpur tried to obtain recognition of his Australian wife, the authorities pointed to Martanda Sydney as an example of why they were so antipathetic to princes marrying white women.

In the early fifties, with her looks fading, Molly was no longer the darling of society. The men who had once madly pursued her were growing old and Molly began increasingly to live in the past. By this time she and Martanda were reconciled and he had come to live with her. Martanda, too, favoured earlier times. It was the old days, the days of perfect manners, where men and women dressed in fine clothes and surrounded themselves with beautiful things, that appealed to the two of them.

By 1952, when Ray McNicoll came to work for Molly, she was drinking too much, mostly gin, which sent her into spirals of deep depression. Maria O'Shea, her devoted maid, said Molly once stayed indoors for three months, spending the entire time in front of the television. Ray noticed a hard edge to Molly, like someone 'who had been around a lot'. Ray would accompany her when she went shopping, bringing up the rear so as to warn Molly when her bag was hanging open or to give her an arm to lean on when her gait became unsteady. 'A bit confused, a bit weary and cranky from the gin,' Molly still insisted on frequenting shops such as Harrods and Fortnum and Masons. Despite these shopping expeditions, Ray found Molly's flat a bit 'drab' and thought Molly 'down on her luck'. Ray considered Molly 'not of this world'; certainly her blase attitude to servants reflected she was not in touch. When Ray began working for Molly and asked what her duties were, Molly 'just waved her hands around telling me to look after the clothes'. When Molly took off for the Riviera at one point she neglected to leave any money for Ray or Maria, yet was put out when one of her friends arranged another job for Ray.

By the 1960s, while the young of London were swinging to the Beatles' tunes, Molly had turned seventy and was living a solitary life, save for her son, Maria and her adored Pekinese dogs. She had become inclined to mythologize her past, and had led Maria to believe that she had spent some seven years in India. Back in Australia, her sister Ida was living alone in a small flat in Sydney, and her brother Ossie, who had once shown so much promise, had become so reclusive he drove his wife to suicide.

In early 1967, Molly was diagnosed with bowel cancer. The prince and Maria took it in turns to care for her. In October Martanda took a break from the sickroom to attend the Shah of Iran's coronation in Teheran. The Shah had not forgotten his old friend and gave him a privileged position at the festivities.

He returned to London to find Molly dying. Despite her condition, she managed to organize the donation of her impressive wardrobe to the Bath Museum of Costume. Summoning all her strength, Molly decided she wished to return to Cannes, which held such happy memories for her. It was

Molly Fink in the 1950s

the scene of her social triumphs. It was where she and the rajah had promenaded along the waterfront together, swinging their young son between them. In Cannes, on 20 November, the rani of Pudukkottai breathed her last. Her grieving son arranged for her ashes to be interred at Golders Green, beside his father's. Seventeen years later his own ashes would be laid to rest beside theirs.

In January 1984, in a room in Florence's elegant Hotel de la Ville, Martanda Sydney died of heart failure. On a bedside table beside him were candles and a small vase of flowers semicircling a photograph of a beautiful woman in furs and pearl pendant earrings. In the corner of the room was a leather travelling case with many small drawers. Within each drawer was an exquisite ornament or jewel – in one there was a huge emerald, in another pearls. This was Molly's final legacy.

Martanda left small legacies to his Sydney friends and the bulk of his estate to the People's Dispensary for Sick Animals. The Indian side of his family successfully contested the will and obtained a share of his legacy. They are still seeking assets of his that they believe are locked away in Swiss banks and in the US.

MORAG MURRAY
married Syed Abdullah of Koh Fort

Scotswoman Morag Murray told the story of her marriage to Syed Abdullah, a Pathan chieftan's son, in her autobiography, published in 1934. The story begins in 1916. Devastated by her brother's death in the First World War on France's killing fields, Morag lost the creative impulse that had led her to paint and decided to do voluntary work. It was at a function associated with this work that she met Syed Abdullah Khan, who was a student at the University of Edinburgh.

Syed was tall with finely chiselled features and had the air of a swashbuckler about him. His manners were impeccable. Morag must have impressed him too, for he offered to drive her home. As he helped her from the car and said goodbye, he took her hand and kissed it. For Morag this was heady stuff.

The next day he sent her a note asking if she would meet him for tea at Mackie's, a popular restaurant on Edinburgh's Princess Street. They enjoyed each other's company so much that they arranged to meet every day thereafter, spending much of their time playing golf in the Braid Hills.

They had not known each other long before Syed proposed. Morag's father James was horrified. He had intended that Morag marry the son of his best friend. Her aunt announced that if Morag forgot about Syed and agreed to marry the boy chosen by her father then Morag would inherit her fortune. Otherwise it would be left to a home for stray cats. Morag told her aunt she could leave her money to whomever she liked – she was going to marry the handsome Pathan.

James Murray felt he knew these eastern types. Syed would undoubtedly be married already, he told Morag. Further, if she married Syed she would be forced to act as a slave to him and his family. Syed would eventually lapse into degenerate Oriental ways, said James, and Morag would be murdered by ground glass mixed into her food. Friends also warned Morag against the marriage, saying that 'Orientals lived in mud huts, were half clad, heathen, and no better than wild savages.'

Syed, for his part, was told that Western women danced and drank and flirted with other women's husbands. Syed's father, who was strongly opposed to the union, cabled asking Morag if she came from a Highland clan of warriors and whether, if called upon, she was able to hold the fort. He softened, however, when Morag agreed to become a Muslim and cabled back his permission for the couple to marry.

James Murray was not so easily persuaded. Not only was his daughter marrying a man of a different race and culture but she was forsaking the faith of her people. It took three months before he was finally won around.

Morag's wedding was a simple affair conducted in the Murrays' dining room. Three Muslims were required at the ceremony: one to act as priest and the other two as witnesses. Three times Morag was asked, 'Do you take this man Syed Abdullah, son of Chieftain Secunder Khan, as your husband, and do you accept a thousand pounds as your dowry?' After Morag's assent, her father read a chapter from the Koran.

A year after their marriage, Morag gave birth to a daughter, Margaret. A year and a half later, Morag, Syed and Margaret set off for Syed's father's domain in what the British called 'No Man's Land' – an eight-hundred-mile corridor of land between Chinese Turkhestan in the north and Baluchistan in the south, which separated India from Afghanistan. They travelled by sea to Karachi, where Margaret's Scottish nurse left them and Morag engaged an Indian hillwoman to take her place. They then made their way to Peshawar, which took them two days. When they reached Peshawar Morag put on a white burqa so that she could roam freely in the city's bazaars and myriad alleyways bustling with activity. From Peshawar they travelled through the Khyber Pass into 'No Man's Land',

> ... one of the least known and most remarkable countries in the world – a strip of land neither India nor Afghanistan, inhabited by clans who owe allegiance to none but their own chiefs, and live in loopholed towers, always armed and sleeping with their rifles at their sides.

The seventy-eight clans of the region, each of which consisted of several thousand people, warred among themselves even more than they did against intruders. A clan chieftain's house would be in the middle of a village, surrounded by high walls with watchtowers at the corners and gateways that were closed and bolted at dusk.

Caravans passed through this forbidding country, taking fruit, nuts, fat-tailed sheep and hill-bred ponies to India to trade. Water was scarce and vegetation sparse but the land was passionately loved by its inhabitants, who called it the 'Free Land of the Hills'. The British admired the fearless and unconquered Pathans and were loath to enter the region. When they did so, they put themselves at great peril. It was because Russia had designs on India, Britain's most prized possession, that Britain attempted to control this buffer zone, and the Afghan Wars were the result.

Savage and patriarchal, the Frontier was not for the faint-hearted. When Morag rode through the turnstile that gave entry to 'No Man's Land,' she turned to her husband and said, 'Syed, I trust you. You realize I am friendless here and have only you.'

Syed replied, 'You and I are together always, Morag. So long as I live, I promise to protect you with my life.'

At the far side of the turnstile they were met by a party of horsemen and escorted to the house of a local khan, where they rested and had a meal. Morag was taken into the women's quarters and plied with questions – the women had never seen a Westerner before. Ten of the khan's men, knives and guns dangling from their belts, then escorted them on the final stage of the journey to Koh Fort – a huge black building with high towers at each corner. Here they were welcomed by Secunder Khan, a solid man with an overpowering personality who stood six foot six tall.

Soon after their arrival, Syed and Morag experienced a wedding celebration that was very different from their mar-riage in Edinburgh. In readiness for the ceremony, Morag bathed in a mixture of asses' milk and rosewater and her hair was massaged with rare henna-coloured oil scented with sandal-wood. Her face, neck, arms and hands were massaged with a traditional concoction, propriety being observed by an elderly woman massaging her legs and arms. A stone was rubbed over her body in a different form of massage and she then took another bath. This time the bath was filled with a heavily scented milky substance that formed a hard pack which was softened with rosewater, then removed. Finally her nails were stained with henna.

A long-sleeved, three-quarter jumper of the finest rose-pink velvet was eased over her head to top baggy trousers made of gold cloth. A pink ninon veil of cobweb fineness, sewn with stones and edged with gold lace, was placed over her head. To complete the outfit, she wore gold-embroidered slippers.

Morag was then led to meet the other hill chieftains' wives and daughters who showered her with presents. The oldest chieftain's wife brought her a silver casket which held a long string of pearls with matching bracelets, earrings, head ornaments and rings. Her mother-in-law presented her with gold jewellery studded with rubies, diamonds and emeralds.

The marriage bed was festooned with ropes of roses as the mullah conducted a simple ceremony similar to the one that had taken place in Edinburgh. Morag was now Begum Jan of Koh Fort.

Once the formalities were over, the guests enjoyed a magnificent feast. The array included chicken, discs of roasted meat, bread, whole sheep, roast mutton, saffron-coloured rice, white pudding topped with silver foil, candies, melons, dried mulberries and walnuts.

Though Morag faced stiff opposition to her marriage from family and friends, the fact that Syed was unlikely to become a ruler of importance meant that there were no political repercussions to the marriage.

Following their marriage, Morag and Syed moved ino their own fort set among picturesque hills and protected by tall armed sentries. Being given a separate dwelling was almost certainly in deference to Morag's nationality. Here she 'dressed in ... Eastern clothes, [and] felt like a medieval lady, held at ransom yet thoroughly enjoying the experience'.

Morag was aware that she enjoyed a level of freedom that was denied Syed's female relations. This freedom, allied with her status as Syed's wife, gave Morag the opportunity to glimpse the world of women confined within the harem.

Morag described a neighbouring chief's harem as situated in a large courtyard of five or six acres with a formal garden and a pathway of sycamore trees leading to a fountain. The harem was divided into ten or eleven rooms for the chief's wife, his daughters, daughters-in-law and mother-in-law. Though gilded, it was nevertheless a cage and Morag did not envy its inhabitants.

Syed was devoted to Morag. He was openly affectionate, calling her his bulbul, his nightingale, and gave her much greater independence than most men in his position would have done. In turn, Morag not only embraced Islam but also Syed's country and his way of life, acting with courage and imagination. When her sister-in-law Salima became engaged to the son of the chief of Killa Fort, the women celebrated with an engagement feast marked by displays of shooting, jumping and wrestling. While their attention was focused on these athletic displays a stranger stole into the fort and took off with a splendid Arab horse, one of the engagement gifts. The men rode off in hot pursuit but while they were away the fort was attacked by brigands. Morag and the women held off the assault until the men returned and managed to repulse the brigands. Miraculously, Morag writes, there was no loss of life.

On another occasion when the fort was under attack and Syed and his men were in danger, Morag took advantage of the clansmen's superstition to save the day. She dressed up in long white flowing robes and pretended to be the mythical White Lady – a figure both revered and feared. This caused consternation among the attackers and the raid failed.

Morag's most dangerous adventure took place in Snake Valley. While travelling through this barren territory she was captured by a ferocious old brigand who said he loved her and was intent on marrying her. He locked her away in a room in his decaying fort which writhed with snakes 'brought back from Hindoostan', saying he would not release her until she agreed to become his wife. Ever resourceful, Morag found some rags, knotted them together, lowered herself down from the window and escaped.

Occasionally Morag and Syed ventured down into India. In Delhi they visited the Red Fort, the Moti Masjid and Chandi Chowk. Morag was appalled by Chandi Chowk with its millions of flies and 'emaciated faces, smallpox-pitted faces, faces eaten by disease, crowded round the windows'. But she found a different kind of beauty in the city where

> I felt envious of the carriage of that poor woman carrying a large brass pot on her head. She might have been an empress instead of an 'untouchable'.

Delhi proved a city of wonders. There were 'Sadhus, sellers of potions, one to turn a beautiful woman into a witch, useful for second wives'. And there was the fakir who crossed the Jumna River on the backs of crocodiles. Morag tells how the fakir had such power over these fearsome creatures that he casually ordered his pet crocodile Nazar not to eat an English child who had fallen into the river.

In India Morag and Syed were the guests of the rajah of Dumpur. They, along with two hundred other guests, had been invited to enjoy Dumpur's fine shikar as well as a series of splendid dinners and, of course, the inevitable fancy dress ball. The rajah singled Morag out for a visit to his treasury which overflowed with incomparable treasures. Morag was shown

> ... old silver armour set with gems, coats of mail diamond studded, helmets with huge rubies, gold vases inlaid with diamonds, goblets encrusted with rubies, cups and saucers of solid silver, gemmed footstools, gold shoes with diamond studded heels,

sapphire-studded spurs, 22 gorgeously jewelled outfits for elephants each worth 50,000 pounds. Cases
of loose pearls, diamonds, rubies, sapphires, opals,
armchairs with pearls and diamonds, gold dinner
service.

Despite all his fabulous jewels, however, the rajah of Dumpur
was particularly taken with the simple set of Scottish pearls
that Morag was wearing. Morag writes that strangely, when
leaving Dumpur, she found her Scottish pearls missing.

Syed and Morag then travelled on to Simla where they had
rented a house for the season. Simla did not appeal to Morag.
She found it peopled by odd characters and cursed by inclem-
ent weather: in June it was swept by a ferocious monsoon. She
was appalled by people's snobbery: 'India is still a land of
slavery, where the fetishes of etiquette and class snobbery rule
despotically and are worshipped by fanatical devotees'. That
snobbery was epitomized by members of the Indian Civil
Service. She writes,

> It is true that there is in India no fence of barbed
> wire between the English people who matter and
> those who do not, but there might well be, for the
> cleavage is deep enough.

As one of those marginalized whites who were not welcomed in the hills, Morag undoubtedly experienced the bite
of that barbed wire fence herself.

After spending some months in Scotland nursing her sick
mother Morag found herself eager to return home. Friends
and relatives' ignorance and prejudice about the Free Land
irritated her, as did her gaping female relations with their
requests for 'harem stories'.

The problems with East-West marriages, Morag felt, arose because the marriages were contracted between unequals. Many alliances between Eastern men and white women were the result of the men 'falling prey to women of the wrong class'. Morag's view was exceptional, for according to the prevailing stereotype interracial marriages occurred because black men lusted after naive and innocent young white women. Morag yearned for the day when East and West would meet on an equal footing. Knowing she was out of step with popular opinion she made an impassioned plea for an ending to racial intolerance and inequality:

> Some day, perhaps long after the bonfires welcom-
> ing us back to the 'Free land' beyond the Khyber
> have blazed and died, other bonfires may proclaim,
> even as our beloved poet Robert Burns so gloriously
> recorded it, 'Man to man the world o'er shall brothers
> be'. May it be so! Inshallah – if Allah wills!

NANCY MILLER

married Maharajah Tukoji Rao Holkar of Indore

*I*ndore, a large wealthy region in central India, owes its origins to Malhar Rao Holkar, a son of humble parents who was born in the village of Hol in 1694. Destiny marked him out as a young man when, as he slept minding his uncle's flocks, a cobra raised its hood and sheltered him from the sun's rays. At the age of thirty, Malhar Rao entered the service of the Peshwa, chief of the Marathas, and eight years later became the commander-in-chief of the Peshwa's armies. For heroic services rendered he received the province of Indore – a region that covered nine thousand square miles and had a population of 850,000.

The Holkar dynasty was commonly believed to be eccentric. During the time of Viceroy Lord Curzon, Maharajah Shivaji Rao Holkar would position himself at a high window and order the abduction of all passers-by who were wearing black coats. At one time he had the bankers of Indore harnessed to the state coach, climbed up on the box himself and drove them around the city. The great imperial adventurer Sir Francis Younghusband, Resident of Indore during Shivaji Rao's reign, found the maharajah a trial. Shivaji Rao announced to Younghusband that he hated the British, although he had a great personal attachment to Queen Victoria. 'He said that some people spoke of her as an ugly old woman but [he] saw she had the light of God in her. To be in her presence was like being in a temple.'

At times Younghusband had to prevent the maharajah from breaches of protocol. On one occasion when they were lined up to greet the duke of Connaught, Shivaji Rao lunged forward to shake the duke's hand and was only prevented from doing so by the diminuitive Sir Francis grabbing him by the coattails. 'The coattails were of the most gorgeous silk,' Sir Francis observed, 'but they held, and the situation was saved. By such resourcefulness do British officers keep the Empire together!'

Englishwoman Violet Jacob provides an evocative description of Shivaji Rao taking part in a Dussehra procession, writing of him sitting 'in a heap like a great toad with blue goggles and an old yellow handkerchief round its neck'. She was surprised to discover that the ugly toad was the maharajah.

In 1903, fed up with Shivaji Rao's behaviour, Sir Francis was ordered to depose him and install his young son Tukoji Rao II as ruler, with Chief Minister Nanak Chand acting as regent. Tukoji Rao proved little better than the father. He was, according to Violet Jacob, 'a light brown child and I should think a horrid brat, resplendent in a pink silk coat with gold buttons, scarlet socks with white spots and yellow shoes. This was crowned by a small black cap like a pill-box.' She described him as an 'an unmannerly goblin'.

Sir Kenneth Fitze, who took over from Younghusband as Resident of Indore, also had a poor opinion of Tukoji. He spoke of him as 'a dangerous lunatic keeping himself under control'. Many of Tukoji's well-documented actions seem to support the Resident's opinion. Suspicious of disloyalty on the part of some members of the Dube family, he casually confiscated the Indore Carriage Works, which belonged to them. He dissolved the marriage of his prime minister because he was epileptic. The prime minister's divorced wife complained:

Nobody can do things that His Highness has done in the whole of the British Empire. After all it is the British army that keeps His Highness on his gaddi. If that protection was withdrawn, the people of Indore would settle the question in a week.

It was the Bawla case, however, that was Tukoji's undoing. A young dancing girl, Mumtaz Begum, was brought to perform for him on one of his visits to Bombay. Tukoji was infatuated. He set Mumtaz up in a palace in Indore along with her mother, Wazir Begum, and relations for company. Her name was changed to the Hindu Kamabai Saheba and she became the maharajah's favourite. Eager to improve her family's position, Wazir Begum planned to get Tukoji to marry the girl, but this was out of the question. Wazir Begum then began looking elsewhere for a more compliant lover.

Tukoji, sensing that something was afoot, had Mumtaz abducted from where she was staying in Bombay and brought back to Indore. Two years later, when Mumtaz was about to give birth, Tukoji summoned Wazir Begum to attend her, as is the Indian custom. Mumtaz had a baby girl and was told that the baby had died.

Broken hearted and suspicious about her baby's death, Mumtaz was easily persuaded by her mother to run away. Soon after, Mumtaz became the mistress of a rich merchant in Bombay. Tukoji's minions, however, were keeping a close watch on her, waiting for the opportunity to return her to the maharajah.

Wazir Begum decided the best way to protect her daughter was to give her to Abdul Kadir Bawla, a rich and politically powerful businessman. Bawla set Mumtaz up in a luxurious flat at Bombay's Chowpatty Beach.

One evening when Mumtaz and Bawla were out for an evening drive on Malabar Hill, a vehicle containing five men appeared and rammed their car. A scuffle followed, during which Bawla was shot dead and his chauffeur injured. One of the assailants, caught by a passing British officer, turned out to be a member of the Indore State Police. Then a second was caught and found to be Tukoji's aide-de-camp.

The case was a sensation, resulting in much publicity both in India and abroad. The attackers were hanged. Tukoji managed to evade the law but was eventually called upon either to abdicate or face an enquiry. Thinking the British had incriminating evidence against him, he stepped down in 1926, but retained the title of maharajah. Mumtaz gave birth to Bawla's daughter and in due course left for Hollywood to make her fame and fortune.

Nancy Miller of Indore, alongwith Joan Falkiner of Palanpur, disproved the British theory that only women of the lower classes would marry Indian princes.

Nancy Miller was born on 9 September 1907 in Seattle, Washington, the daughter of a concert pianist mother and a businessman father who owned gold mines in Alaska. She tells, 'My father fell in love with my mother when she was playing at a piano recital. It was love at first sight.' Nancy believed in such cataclysmic love.

Nancy was given a convent education, going on to the University of Washington where she studied Oriental civilisation. Every year she travelled abroad with her family. Her grandfather, Mr Schaeffer, was French, and her grandmother Swiss: both considered it necessary for a girl of good breeding to become familiar with European culture. Nancy was never expected to work for a living.

Nancy Miller and Tukoji Rao Holkar met at the Le Kursall Casino in Lausanne, Switzerland, where Nancy was visiting with her grandparents. Tukoji was in Switzerland staying at his villa. Infatuated with the young woman, Tukoji pursued her to Paris and then back home to the US. Before long he summoned up the courage to ask her grandfather's permission for them to marry. No doubt he was concerned that the scandal of the Bawla case might have prejudiced the Schaeffers against him. Mr Schaeffer, however, was an indulgent grandfather, and he asked Nancy what she wanted to do. She told him that she was in love with the maharajah.

It was decided that Nancy's grandmother would accompany her to India as chaperone. They spent Christmas on board the *S.S. Genoa* and docked in Bombay on 26 December 1927. There they were met by the American consul who had been briefed by the British to warn Nancy against marrying the maharajah.

It was a delicate situation. Nancy was an American, and the US was a stern critic of Britain's imperial interests. The British were worried about the American press taking up the case. They were not concerned about reading the riot act to Tukoji but they had to treat Nancy with kid gloves. She was described by the Resident as a woman of 'great charm and goodness amounting to piety. She was a good influence on him.'

Although Tukoji had been persuaded to abdicate in favour of his son Yeshwant, the people of Indore still thought of Tukoji as their father and mother. In their eyes he had done nothing to break the bond linking prince and people. It was their British overlords who baulked at murder. Indians generally saw murder and maiming, plunder and torture as unexceptional. Rajahs and maharajahs had been doing it for hundreds of years. It was often the very means whereby they initially obtained their right to rule. But Tukoji's decision to marry a white woman was another matter altogether. In his subjects' eyes, such a marriage might well sever the reciprocity between ruler and ruled.

His own caste in particular were vehement: they did not want a white woman as their maharani. Tukoji thundered, threatening to change his religion. He threatened Indian guests who refused to attend the wedding. He told members of his own subcaste, the Dhangars, that when his son came of age they would be punished for their opposition to his marriage.

His two maharanis, the senior and junior, received the news of his impending marriage with horror. The junior maharani went on a prolonged hunger strike in an attempt to stop the marriage. To rub salt into the wound, the maharanis were told by Tukoji that they had to attend the wedding. Nancy was blithely unaware of the maharanis' opposition, however, and believed Tukoji when he told her they were happy to have her as a 'sister'.

The British tried another tactic to stop the wedding. They threatened to reduce Tukoji's fifty-thousand-pound allowance. He was unconcerned. They warned their officials to stay away from the wedding. They then sought legal advice as to Hindu law. They ascertained that the marriage was legal according to the Sudra custom. What concerned them most, however, was their own law which decreed that any children born after the abdication would not be recognized in the succession.

A week before the wedding Nancy converted to Hinduism under the guidance of the revered sage, Sri Sankaracharya, and her name was changed to Sharmistha Devi. The English Indian press suggested the conversion was a sham and wrote of it as being 'staged'.

Tukoji invited a thousand guests from outside Indore to attend his wedding. The bigger the event and the greater the number of prominent guests that attended, the greater the chance of it being recognized. He asked the British for the use of Indore's state elephants, its troops, its horses and bands. Assent was given, but it was confirmed that no important British official would attend.

On 17 March 1928 at Daryava Palace in Barwaha, Nancy and Tukoji were married. It was an evening ceremony conducted according to Maratha custom, held in a large open-sided tent pitched outside the palace. Amid fireworks and brilliant lights, Nancy walked to her appointed place accompanied by Colonel Lambhate. Several Europeans and Parsis were present. So too were representatives from the princely states of Kohlapur and Bhopal, as well as ones from a number of smaller states who looked on with considerable curiosity. Various prominent nobles of Indore also, in the end, decided to attend. Tukoji's subjects rightly feared his ill temper.

Tukoji and Nancy arrived at the pavilion from opposite directions, then sat facing each other, Tukoji facing east and Nancy facing west. He was dressed as a Maratha nobleman of the First Class, wearing the unusual Maratha headdress resembling a quarter moon laid on its side. Nancy wore a brocaded Benares sari of real gold thread that was almost too heavy for her slight frame to support. She was assisted by Tukoji's sisters and other female members of the Holkar family, but his maharanis were spared the final humiliation of having to participate in the ceremonial preparations.

After the marriage knot was tied, Tukoji and Nancy ascended the dais where the sacrificial fire, the havan, was worshipped. Then they left the tent to travel through the balmy night, the loud and vibrant procession slowly making its way to the palace where the Lakshmi Puja, worship of the Goddess of Wealth, concluded the marriage ceremonies.

Nancy soon adjusted to having numerous servants around her. She had five ladies-in-waiting who were her companions, five maidservants to bathe her, help her dress and look after her clothes, and there were five cooks in the kitchen. She became accustomed to silver vessels being used for bathing and at meal times and the obeisance, forehead touching the ground, performed by her servants when they entered the room.

Tukoji's annual income of fifty thousand pounds, following his abdication, was reputedly equal to the combined incomes of the kings of Denmark, Norway and Bulgaria. His collection of cars and jewels epitomized the wealth he had at his disposal. He and Nancy had a Rolls Royce, a large Packard, a small Packard, a Delage and a Chrysler, while his Indian wives enjoyed a similar selection of cars based upon their rank. His senior maharani had a Rolls Royce, the junior maharani a Buick and Tukoji's daughter a Sunbeam. In addition to the luxury cars there were three service cars, a companion Brake, a servant's Brake and a Fiat.

The Indore toshakhana was noted for its magnificent jewels, the most valuable being a necklace of 43 emeralds, a necklace of 199 diamonds and 5 emeralds, a pair of diamond and emerald bangles, one turban ornament of 2 big emeralds and 1 big diamond, one turban ornament studded with diamonds, a necklace of matchless diamonds and emeralds, buttons of diamonds and rubies, a 5-string pearl necklace, a 9-string pearl necklace, a 7-string pearl necklace with 700 pearls, pearl earrings and a nose ring studded with diamonds and pearls.

When he abdicated, Tukoji handed over most of Indore's palaces and treasure to his son. All save Sukh Niwas, the Daryava Mahal in Barwaha, and the magnificent Lalbagh Palace with its gilded archways, its columned banquetting hall dominated by a huge cut-glass chandelier, its durbar room with its ceiling fresco of angels and seraphim drawing chariots breasting cotton-wool clouds, and its park-like gardens dotted with Italian marble cherubs. A blend of Renaissance and Baroque styles, the palace is considered one of the most elegant residences in India. This was Tukoji and Nancy's home and where they raised their four daughers.

As maharani, Nancy was an unqualified success, involving herself in a wide range of activities and by degrees winning over family members. She struggled to master Hindi, under the tutelage of a pandit employed by Tukoji, but had limited success. She even employed a unique strategy to learn the language: she would give speeches in Hindi transcribed into English script with French accents. Tukoji still played a minor role in Indore state affairs and Nancy as his consort appeared at sports presentations, religious functions and the opening of hospitals and schools. She was as well versed as he in the Holkar family's long and turbulent history and spent much of her time committing the state's and family's history to permanent record.

She was a keen sportswoman, being particularly fond of tennis and riding. Like most members of the ruling elite she took up shikar and used to venture out into the jungle on elephant back, but she was so upset after shooting a tiger cub that she gave up the sport and never shot again.

She kept busy with family gatherings and picnics, and with entertaining the many guests who were drawn to Indore because of this energetic and charming woman being the Lalbagh's chatelaine. Later, when her stepson Yeshwant married Fay Crane she became a friend and confidante to the younger woman, and a shoulder to cry on when the situation became particularly difficult with Yeshwant's drug and alcohol consumption.

Nancy loved animals and she had a menagerie of pets that further filled her busy schedule. She kept up her piano playing and built up an extensive collection of classical records. She loved visiting the markets but in deference to her position and out of respect for her husband, when she travelled through Indore she kept herself in purdah, with the shutters of her car firmly shut.

In order to escape overseas from what they considered to be their rather tedious lives in India, the princes lied to the British, feigned illness and concocted pressing family obligations. Tukoji was no exception. He boldly told the Resident of Indore that his doctor had told him to lead a 'gay life' in Paris and he was following the prescribed treatment faithfully. He and Nancy went to the races, gambled at the casinos, went to nightclubs and generally lived the life of the idle .rich, mixing with other Indian royals such as the Palanpurs. For several months each year the Holkars took up residence at their villa at Cap Ferat in the south of France. Their neighbour was deposed empress Farah Diba of Iran. Here, like many of India's princes (including the nawab of Palanpur), they held lavish parties and visited the casinos and local nightclubs.

In addition to the Lalbagh and Sukh Niwas palaces in Indore and the Daryava Mahal at Barwaha, Nancy and Tukoji owned a house on the outskirts of Paris in Saint Germain. It was so lavish it was said to 'make the members of the old French nobility who are his [Tukoji's] neighbours look like paupers'.

In Tukoji's last years he became bedridden from a broken hip. He and Nancy would have their meals together. She would play the piano for him and together they would watch the feeding of the peacocks.

Their daughters and their families were attentive and the palace was always full of visitors. There were tragedies but they bore them together: their beloved granddaughter was killed

Nancy Miller at Sukh Niwas in 1992

in an Air India plane crash. Nancy nursed Tukoji's daughter from the senior maharani when she was dying of tuberculosis and it was in her arms the twenty-year-old breathed her last.

Nancy was devoted to Tukoji and considered their marriage an unqualified success. When he died on 27 May 1978 she was devastated. She never considered moving back to America. 'Why go to America,' she said, 'and live all alone in a condominium?'

Following Tukoji's death Nancy moved into the smaller palace, the Sukh Niwas. She continued to involve herself in Indore's municipal matters, in the conservation of its heritage and its water resources. She kept fit and mentally alert.

In October 1992 I travelled to Indore to see Maharani Sharmistha Devi (Nancy's Indian name) – the last European woman during British times to thumb her nose at convention and marry her Indian prince despite his reputation. Elegantly dressed in a sari, she was warm and friendly. Her face was lined but her complexion was still as white as the alabaster of the vases that dotted her palace. Servants came and went. While they were in awe of the maharani it was clear that they also loved her. Her grandson, who had just returned from Bombay, came to pay his respects. Forehead to the floor, he touched her feet deferentially. He filled her in on the latest family news, touched her feet again and departed.

At the time, Nancy was in the process of building a white marble and red granite chhatriya (cenotaph) to Tukoji. On her death she planned to be cremated at his cremation ground and have a modest slab to her memory placed near his grander monument.

Five years later I was flicking through a society magazine and came across a headline 'Royal Tussle'. I read that following Nancy's death there were rumours that her daughter Sharada Raje had poisoned her and that as a result an autopsy was performed on the maharani's body. 'There was no dignified mourning,' said a member of the family regretfully. Since then there has been bitter fighting between Nancy's daughters' families over her will and many of the treasures bequeathed to her by Tukoji have turned up in Bombay's antique shops.

MOLLIE ELSIP

married Prince Ali Khan of Jaora

*M*ollie Elsip grew up with two brothers and two sisters in Tetbury where her father was a travelling salesman for a Gloucestershire firm. Her mother kept an elegant dress shop and her customers included the duchess of Beaufort, Lady Helena Gibb, Lady Holford and the countess of Westmorland.

It was while Mollie was working in a draper's shop in Cirencester that she was introduced by a mutual friend to Prince Nasir Ali Khan of Jaora. Jaora was a state of middling importance situated in central India, with a population of seventy-six thousand, and had been given a salute of thirteen guns by the British.

Nasir had been sent to England to study at Cirencester's Royal Agricultural College. That first meeting was followed by a daily rendezvous: they went dancing, to the theatre, on picnics and motoring in the Cotswold countryside. Accomplished at sports, Nasir was a popular figure at Cirencester and captained the college cricket team. He and Mollie played tennis together and he taught her to play golf.

Nasir had just scraped through his first year at college. During his second year, after meeting Mollie, he failed his exams. He also failed his final year, and it was suggested that he had deliberately done so in order to have an excuse to remain with Mollie. This suspicion was confirmed when Mollie, aged twenty-one, and Nasir, aged twenty-five, married at

Woking Mosque in December 1930. Nasir continued to live at the college and Mollie at home until, six months later, a second registry office wedding took place to confirm the marriage according to English law.

In March 1931, Mollie discovered she was pregnant and decided that it was time to tell her parents that she and Nasir were married. Her father James was reconciled to the fact but her mother was horrified. In June that year the young couple moved into a small, attractive villa in Reading, and in November 1931 their daughter, Margaret Dolores, was born. At that point Mollie and her mother were reconciled.

In February 1932, the British press got hold of the story. The *Daily Sketch* headlined details of the unusual marriage, Nasir telling the story in his own words. He explained that the presence of an English nurse, governess and guardian during his upbringing had given him a preference for the English, although he conceded that at one time he had said he was opposed to mixed marriages. He said that from his earliest days in England he had wanted to win an English wife. He defended his right to marry Mollie, explaining that he was opposed to multiple wives and that love and religion were the two pre-eminent factors in his life. In his words 'I like the chariot of my life to be drawn by two horses together – "Love" and "Religion".'

He said that they were continuing to live in England because life in Jaora would be too difficult for Mollie. He said the absence of theatre, cinema and dancing (only available a hundred miles away at the army base of Mhow), the interests he and Mollie shared together, would make life particularly difficult for 'the Begum'. Two other aspects of life in India had to be considered as well: 'the Indian climate was hostile to an English girl,' and the sequestration imposed by purdah. Though in major cities like Bombay, Calcutta and Delhi, Mollie might move about freely, in Muslim Jaora, the capital of his father's state, Mollie would have to conform to tradition.

The more crucial fact was that Nasir's father disapproved of the marriage. When Nawab Iftikhar Ali Khan of Jaora first heard of the marriage he implored Nasir to return to India alone. Nasir said that he would not return unless Mollie was welcomed as well. If she wasn't, then, he told his father, 'I stay by my wife in England'. He said he was willing to take up any job for which his agricultural knowledge and love of sport equipped him. There were few.

The birth of Margaret Dolores eased the tensions between Nasir and his father. In November 1932 the *Daily Sketch* noted, 'All's Well in Secret Romance. Indian Prince Sails with Shopgirl Wife. Father Forgives.'

When Mollie arrived in Jaora accompanied by her sister, they set about spending lavish sums of money on themselves and their friends. Mollie could see no harm in this, given that the Jaora royal family had long indulged its own whims without regard to the condition of their subjects. Superintendent of Police Leslie Robbins wrote of the nawab housing his dogs in air-conditioned kennels 'while the wretched people alongside them were half starved'. Notwithstanding the nawab's scant concern for them, his subjects were prepared to accept almost anything from their ruler – but not his English daughter-in-law. She was not a daughter of the soil; she was not one of their own.

Leslie Robins noted the fears that were held for the safety of Mollie and her sister when they arrived in Jaora. Robins writes:

> The danger was that these English girls would be poisoned. Every Viceroy, during his tour of duty, came to Central India and this involved having

Mollie Elsip married Prince Ali Khan of Jaora

breakfast at Jaora State. When Willingdon came
Lady Willingdon accompanied him ... she sent for
the Nawab and said, 'I hold you responsible for
these girls. If anything happens to them you will
have to deal with me.' She put the fear of God into
the old Nawab and I think that was one reason why
they weren't poisoned. Various factions of the State
didn't like the heir marrying an English woman. I
wouldn't have put it beyond him to poison them
himself in the end. We were in touch with them.

Though the nawab preferred to spend his money on dogs
and fishing, when Mollie and Nasir came to live in Jaora he
provided the funds for a magnificent palace to be built for
them by John Roberts of Bombay in the grounds of his own
Machobhi Bhawan. It seemed a fitting way for an English
princess to begin her married life in India. Built in the most
modern and lavish style, it failed, however, to compensate
Mollie for a marriage that soon turned sour.

Jaora's ruling family had many European visitors, including
the viceroy and vicereine of India. Mollie and her sister cringed
at such visits. For a start Mollie was embarrassed by her father-
in-law's bizarre methods of entertaining his guests. He would
challenge his visitors to name any breed of dog and then
proceeded to produce an example from his kennels, much as
a conjuror pulls rabbits out of a hat. When it came to eccentric
behaviour, however, the nawab's paled in comparison to that
of his son, Mollie's husband.

Nasir complained to Jaora's political agent that 'the condition of the zenana was worse than that which obtained in
Alwar during the late maharajah's time'. The political agent
wrote to his senior officer that as 'I know something of that
unhappy time, we can confidently say, if Nasir is to be believed,

that the present state of the Jaora Zenana must be indescribable.' In an annexure the agent added that the 'sexual promiscuity of Jaora appears to beat most records'.

The authorities soon discovered that Nasir's claims about the harem were a smokescreen for his own behaviour. Not only had he been using police officials to procure young girls, he had also been visiting his father's harem on the pretext of seeing his father's wives on business. The political agent's spies reported that the zenana was also much favoured by Mollie's brother-in-law Murtaza, who would raid its chests of diaphanous silks and beaded chiffons to 'dress exotically', while her other brother-in-law Usman, who 'had a partiality for lipstick', visited the zenana to exchange cosmetic tips with his father's concubines.

Margaret Dolores' birth was followed by that of two boys, Robin and David. Mollie found herself having to be both mother and father to the children as Nasir was far too busy amusing himself in the harem. He was also busy devising ways to intimidate his father, threatening to have him murdered if he did not name Nasir as his heir.

Nasir's father had succeeded to the gaddi in 1883. His senior begum died childless in 1918. His second wife, Mumtaz Mahal, was a Hindu of low caste who had converted to Islam on marriage. In 1906 Mumtaz gave birth to Nasir followed by another son, Entesham, and then in 1914, came the twins, Usman and Murtaza. (She also had three daughters whose status is exemplified by the fact that in the records, they remain nameless.) As the nawab officially married Mumtaz in 1914, only the twins were legitimate. Out of the blue, however, the nawab 'remembered' that he had secretly married Mumtaz in 1905 and therefore all his sons were legitimate. The British dismissed this as a 'try on'. Later, in 1942, the nawab admitted that this had been a lie that Nasir had forced him to come up with, saying that he would otherwise kill him.

To escape her difficult circumstances in Jaora, Mollie would sometimes visit Mussoorie where she could socialise with other Europeans, some of whom were themselves married to Indian princes. At Jagatjit Singh's magnificent Chateau de Kapurthala, these European women were free to wear their Western clothes and indulge in European pastimes that were frowned upon in their husbands' states. Mollie could dance, roller-skate, and attend the theatre without the censure of her husband's Muslim subjects. When her marriage to Nasir Khan was falling apart it was in Mussoorie that Mollie found solace. Leslie Robbins writes in *Policing the Raj* that it was here that Mollie met and fell in love with a British officer.

Nasir took few pains to hide his debauched behaviour from anyone, least of all his wife. Mollie worried about the influence he was having on the children and her visits to England became increasingly frequent. Her father-in-law agreed to funds being put aside to enable her to live in England and in 1939 she packed her bags and with her three children left India for good for a country house, Spinner Close, in Somming, Berkshire. In 1941 she had her last communication with Nasir.

In England Mollie found much was made of her 'exotic-ness': she was photographed by Marcus Adams for *The Tatler* and *The Illustrated Weekly of India*. She enrolled Robin at Marlborough College despite the fact that Nasir was running up huge debts. Nasir tried to get her allowance redirected to himself but the nawab interceded, directing that Mollie's allowance be drawn on the Jaora state treasury and sent directly to her in England. Despite the nawab's diligence in ensuring that Mollie was properly provided for, she was chided by the India Office for not even bothering to write a short note to her father-in-law telling him about his grandchildren.

In 1943 Nasir was banished from Jaora because of his involvement in rioting that had thrown his state into turmoil. He left for Mussoorie with his brother Usman's divorced wife, married her and then divorced her after three months. He then married his stepmother Chota Bi and they moved to Ajmer. This behaviour enraged his father, who never forgave him. In 1945, aged thirty-nine, Nasir died of a heart attack, leaving huge debts. The nawab continued to send Mollie an allowance to pay for the children's education and contributed to the upkeep of her Berkshire home.

STELLA MUDGE

married Paramjit Singh, maharajah of Kapurthala

Stella Mudge's maternal grandparents were farmers in Ilkley, Yorkshire. Stella's father, a wirewalker who performed at country fairs, took lodgings with Stella's grandparents when he was performing with the fair at Ilkley. While living with the family, he and Stella's mother Elsie were mutually attracted. Friendship blossomed into love and soon they were married and Elsie left the farm forever. Their marriage produced five children: Doris, Fred, Stella, Elsie and Betty. Stella was born in Carlton, Kent, on 13 October 1904.

With a wife and young children to support, Stella's father gave up his itinerant life. His first venture into business was a hairdressing shop in London's East End but it lacked the excitement and adulation of the fair. Soon a way to combine wirewalking with a more lucrative trade presented itself. He scraped together his savings and bought a pub in the East End. On the first day of business he put on an exhibition of wirewalking. Hundreds of spectators flocked to see him walk the wire high above the London streets. The pub was an instant success and the Mudges were launched in a business that provided them with a comfortable living.

Stella attended Coburn Grammar School for Girls at Bow where she breezed through her studies and became fluent in French. She studied piano and cello at the Guildhall School of Music and was gifted at painting. At Miss Maclaren's School of Dancing, Stella excelled at ballet and ballroom dancing,

Stella Mudge, pictured here at age thirteen, was ever the performer

Stella Mudge

although her sister Doris was technically more gifted. Betty, Stella's sister, said that their mother maintained that 'Stella would always get the audition as she had all the front'.

Stella's fondness for 'things' was apparent from an early age. During a bombing raid Betty remembers the Mudge family scurrying for their lives, shoeless, with dressing gowns thrown over their nightclothes. All except Stella. She took her time choosing her most valuable possessions and packing them carefully in her jewel box, and only then did she follow the rest of her family to shelter.

With her red hair, bow lips, long slim legs and 'the front' her mother had remarked upon, Stella got a job in the chorus of Jack Hulbert and Cicely Courtnedge's show at London's Little Theatre. Well aware of Stella's waywardness, her mother Elsie made a point of collecting her every night after the show had finished. One evening while Elsie was waiting at the stage door for Stella to emerge, the doorman informed her that the company had gone to Paris.

With Stella underage and unpredictable, Elsie immediately left for Paris to bring her wayward daughter home. This, however, proved impossible. Stella refused to return with her mother 'to boring old England'. She had tasted freedom and was enjoying herself immensely.

One evening promoter Max Rivers came to see the company perform and Stella caught his eye. He was impressed by her looks and extroversion and thought she would be better suited to nightclub cabaret. So he persuaded Stella to leave the show and join the cast of the *Folies Bergere*.

In 1922 Paramjit Singh was at the *Folies Bergere* with his wife Brinda and saw eighteen-year-old Stella performing. She was wearing a long green-sequinned sheath that showed her figure to perfection. Paramjit was smitten and asked to be introduced to the beautiful dancer. He went backstage and

Stella Mudge before her marriage to the maharajah of Kapurthala

presented her with a gorgeous bouquet of flowers and then
followed her when she rejoined Cicely Courtnedge's show and
toured England. When she returned to Paris Paramjit was in
tow and before long he had persuaded Stella to leave the show
and join him at the Ritz Hotel.

Like his father Jagatjit Singh, maharajah of Kapurthala,
Paramjit Singh was cultured and westernized and had a
penchant for things French. He had been educated at Harrow
in England and had then spent two years at the Lycee Janson
de Sailly in Paris. Paramjit stood in his father's shadow and
had been given no state responsibilities. He was a dilettante,
concerned mainly with his own entertainment, as British
officials noted with disdain. Official records note that he was
concerned about arrangements for his amusement rather than
the welfare of his subjects when he made one of his infrequent
tours of the state.

Paramjit's first wife was a high-caste princess from the
Himalayan state of Jubbal. They had been betrothed when she
was seven years old and he nine. Following the betrothal the
young princess Brinda came into the maharajah's care and was
sent off to Paris to be educated. The maharajah was determined that his future daughter-in-law should speak French
and be familiar with French manners and culture, but when
Brinda returned to India to marry Paramjit, Jagatjit found she
had learned more than pretty manners and had a westernized
mind of her own. She was not the acquiescent Indian daughter-
in-law he had hoped for – she spoke contemptuously of his
new wife as 'the Spanish dancer' and failed to provide her
husband with a son. She had three daughters.

In 1919 Stella accompanied Paramjit to India as his mistress.
Paramjit attempted to be discreet about their relationship but
Stella in her usual style would have none of it.

For Stella, life in India was a matter of shuttling between Kapurthala, Simla, Delhi and Mussoorie. She liked India, she felt at home here although less so in Kapurthala where she complained that every servant was a spy and every maid an enemy. Moreover, Jagatjit Singh refused to allow her inside the main palace.

Paramjit built Stella a love nest that she named Stella Cottage and had it fitted out in European style. Compared with most of Kapurthala's palaces the residence was not grand but it suited Stella. Brinda's palace was only three miles away from Stella Cottage but 'fortunately out of earshot of her high-pitched tinkly laugh'. According to Prince Martand Singh, Stella and Paramjit led a lonely existence in Kapurthala until Paramjit persuaded his brothers, each in turn, to invite him and Stella for dinner once a week. They would then return the invitation, which provided them with some social diversion.

Headstrong and fiercely independent, Stella refused to have any maids to wash her hair or dress her, preferring to 'do' for herself, even to the extent of making her own clothes. She didn't trust Indian servants. She described the seventy-two gardeners who tended the lawns of Stella Cottage to her sister Elsie as 'seventy-two enemies'.

In India Stella wore Indian dresses – mostly richly brocaded Benares saris woven with pure gold thread. Many were sheer silk chiffon and Stella often wore them without blouses which shocked the women of the court. They were disgusted by the showy gems she wore with her saris, even in the daytime. She had the pick of the legendary Kapurthala treasury but was never satisfied, so Paramjit set about buying her incomparable pieces from Cartier, Bulgari, Lalique, and Van Clef and Arpels. With her acquisitive habits and 'decidedly East London accent', Brinda's family say they felt cheated 'that she was ever brought to the palace'.

Stella in her Indian finery

Following Brinda's failure to give birth to a son, the maharajah found Paramjit a suitable Rajput girl from Kangra to be his second wife. Paramjit was unwilling to marry the girl, however, dismissing her as 'jungly' and quite unlike his worldly wise Stella.

Ann Morrow writes that well aware of Stella's power over his son, Jagatjit offered her a million rupees to persuade Paramjit to marry the Kangra girl. Stella took the rupees and duly persuaded Paramjit to take the girl as his second wife. It then became a matter of Paramjit consummating the marriage.

Daily the women of the zenana washed and oiled the young bride in scents and unguents, but to no avail. One evening, however, a fierce fight with Stella drove Paramjit to the arms of his long-suffering wife. Trailed by his aide-de-camp carrying his silk pyjamas, Paramjit made his way to the zenana and his waiting bride. Son and heir Sukhjit Singh was conceived that night but Paramjit never visited the zenana again. He and Stella sailed for Europe the next day.

In 1935 when Paramjit and his father attended Italian army manoeuvres hosted by Benito Mussolini, Stella was comfortably ensconced in their Paris apartment where, among other activities, she kept herself amused by playing her two magnificent grand pianos. When Paramjit and Jagatjit continued on to the Nazi Parteitag in Nuremberg, Stella was busy socializing with her friends, among them Betty Ritz who was a member of the famous hotel family.

It was not until July 1937, fifteen years after they had met, that Stella and Paramjit became husband and wife. They married in England's Sikh Gurdwara according to the Sikh Anand Marriage Act. Upon her marriage Stella took the name Narinder Kaur. She wore a heavy gold Benares silk brocade sari and a chamois silk sleeveless blouse complemented by diamond-studded gold jewellery fashioned by Cartier.

Stella Mudge, circa 1948

Maharani Stella was not bothered by official disapproval. It did not bother her that British society looked down on her. She was ignored when the invitations to balls and parties went out but her attitude was 'to hell with it'.

Stella's family derived no satisfaction from her privileged position. She frequently invited them out to India, then at the last moment called to say it was inconvenient for them to come. Her sister Doris had paid for a ticket to India but Stella withdrew the invitation only two days before she was due to fly out. Elsie had wanted to visit Stella in Kapurthala but says she knew she 'could have easily ended up in the kitchen for the duration'.

Throughout their time together Stella and Paramjit were frequently abroad, travelling in style as befitting royalty with Paramjit's aide-de-camp and a bevy of retainers. Paramjit preferred Europe (particularly France) and England to India and it was often he who instigated their many trips. They divided their time between France and England, often returning to Paris. Stella and Paramjit patronized London's best hotels: the Savoy, Claridges and the Dorchester. Stella would travel with as many as ninety-six suitcases, invariably only half of which would return to India. In Europe it was the same. The Kapurthala treasures entered Swiss safety deposit boxes and French and English banks, mostly under aliases: she used five or six different names.

When Stella and Paramjit visited London they had both a big Rolls Royce and a little one. When they went shopping, Stella insisted that the chauffeur park the Rolls around the corner out of sight. She was concerned that if shopkeepers saw the car they 'would charge them double'.

Stella even curbed Paramjit's generosity to her own family. When he wanted to give five pounds to the nanny who had been with the family for thirty years, she said severely, 'Too

Stella and Paramjit on holiday abroad

much', and the nanny was simply given a pound. When she came to visit, Stella bought her family cheap gifts such as tin candlesticks and wooden knick-knacks.

In 1938, following a fight with Paramjit, Stella rented a flat for herself in London. In a gesture of reconciliation she invited Paramjit and her sister Betty to dinner. Stella served stale bread rolls to accompany two pieces of bony chicken that had been boiled with a handful of rice. Paramjit enthused over the meal, gushing, 'Oh Beady [his nickname for Stella], Beady that was beautiful'.

During the Second World War Stella and Paramjit locked themselves away in their Paris apartment and lived, according to Stella, off bread and cheese. Stella persuaded the Nazis to leave her precious possessions alone. Her jewels in the Banque de Paris remained untouched as did the treasures she had in Swiss bank accounts. From time to time she had to make fleeting visits to Zurich.

Stella called Paramjit her 'doggie darling' and kept a gall-stone of his in a glass bottle in her handbag. Paramjit was besotted with Stella and would forgive her anything, although on one occasion she nearly went too far. In 1951, the two of them were invited to a dinner at the home of a duchess. The guests had been talking about Prince Phillip, and Stella said, 'Oh, do you know he's having an affair with ...' Her remark was received with thunderous silence. The duchess raised herself to an imperious height and said to Paramjit, 'Would you mind taking your wife out of my home?'

Mortified, Paramjit escorted Stella from the house. In the street, Stella was so enraged she threw herself down on the pavement kicking and screaming. A passing pedestrian stopped and asked if he could help, thinking Stella was having an epileptic fit. The next day Paramjit took Stella to her mother and said, 'Here madam. I would like to return your daughter to you.' In the end, however, Stella and Paramjit left together.

Stella's effect on society was not always so disastrous. She and Paramjit were invited for an audience with the Dowager Queen Mary who took Paramjit across to a large painting hanging on the wall and pointed to a young boy she said was him as a child.

Stella was often referred to by the British press as the charming Tikka Rani. Her vanity must have been satisfied with another report that described her as the most beautiful princess in India who was often referred to as India's rose. It seems likely that the copy was supplied by Stella herself.

In 1948 Stella and Paramjit visited London for Paramjit to see his daughter, Princess Indira. Indira was free-spirited like her mother Brinda. She enjoyed 'bathing holidays' in Cannes and in 1938 she had appeared on the London stage as a Turkish slave girl. During the war she had driven an ambulance and given talks on BBC radio. She preferred to live in Chelsea in

The maharajah and maharani of Kapurthala

London because, as she explained, 'there is something more to life than just the never-ending Hindu ceremonies and feasts'. Indira and Stella despised each other. (Later Indira fell in love with Prince Duleep Singh of Jamnagar, the famous cricketer. He was a Rajput and she a Sikh, and his family refused to countenance the marriage. Neither ever married.)

At the time, reporters asked Paramjit, who was just about to succeed his father, whether he was very rich and he answered, 'You may, if you like, describe me as a millionaire without the multi.' Most of what Paramjit had, Stella managed to acquire. In Kapurthala, Brinda's family said 'Stella was very acquisitive' and described her as a 'money grubber'. While her father-in-law was alive there was some check on what she managed to remove but when her husband ascended the gaddi she went overboard.

When Paramjit became maharajah in 1948, Stella insisted on a coronation, despite the fact that Independence had swept away the princely states. Stella wearing a tiara designed by Cartier was crowned alongside her husband.

When Paramjit fell ill in 1955 (suffering from melancholia and a nervous breakdown, according to his daughter Ourmila), Stella was kept from his deathbed. His family were determined that she should not get her hands on what was left of his money. The enemies that she had made in his family over the years were at last able to take their revenge. Stella claimed that they forced Paramjit to change his will in their favour just before he died. Brinda 'kicked Stella out of the palace' after she attended Paramjit's funeral. As his body lay in state in Kapurthala palace, Stella stood by the bier dressed in black but outraged the family by wearing bright red lipstick. Princess Ourmila remembers Stella persisting in wearing her beautiful diamonds even when she was in mourning.

Stella was equally despised by the people of Kapurthala. Prince Martand Singh recalls that about this time, before she left the state, Stella and her friend Betty Ritz arrived at his father's house in a cycle rickshaw and asked for money. 'It was given.' The cycle rickshaw man told Prince Karamjit, 'It is only out of respect for your family that I am keeping them in the rickshaw. Otherwise I would have thrown them out.'

As part of the settlement of Paramjit's estate, an inventory was carried out of two chests of Kapurthala treasure, both of which were in Paris – one at the Ritz Hotel and the other at the Chase Bank. Stella was given a tantalizing glimpse of these precious items under the supervision of a French judge. There was a 44-carat turban diamond surrounded by brilliants, 4 pearl necklaces, 200 gold watches, 32 chessmen in gold and coloured enamel, and jewels estimated to be worth five hundred thousand pounds. But the French court ruled that the jewels and the treasure belonged to the maharajah's only son, Col Sukhjit Singh.

Sukhjit also identified a safety deposit box in France that was opened and the majority of its contents awarded to him and his family. Ann Morrow writes 'Stella got nothing and came back to London a bit blowzy from too many gins and oranges.' But that was not entirely true. Stella had got away with far more than anyone realized, including the Kapurthala coronation tiara.

Sukhjit knew that Stella was sitting on a fortune but he did not know how to find it. He discovered that she had fifty trunks stored at the Dorchester Hotel, the storage costs of which had not been paid in years. He took out an order against Stella forcing her to open the trunks in his presence and that of the hotel manager. Stella asked her brother-in-law Bob Bishop to accompany her. For two hours, in slow motion and with theatrical gestures, Stella unpacked various items. First there was a tea strainer, followed by a packet of soap, a hand towel with the Claridges crest on it, then a beaded tea cosy. Finally, one by one, she unpacked a large packet of ladies sanitary napkins. Sukhjit found neither jewels nor the coronation tiara. In fact, Stella had sold the tiara some time before through a well-known London auction house.

Her sister Betty recalls Stella visiting England at about this time and complaining that the Indian government was hounding her for tax. She rang up from London at 1 a.m. asking them to meet her at 3 a.m. at Bromley station. As Bob stood waiting, a carriage door opened and Stella stumbled onto the platform with her arms full of furs – sable, mink and ermine. Her leather trunks tooled with S. Kapurthala were bursting, the locks scarcely able to contain the contents.

'Stella didn't believe in paying income tax,' said Bob. In fact, she did not believe in paying for anything that she could successfully obtain free. Betty recalls an occasion when Stella came to stay with her in Bromley. The three sisters, Elsie, Betty and Stella, went shopping for outfits for Elsie's son's wedding. They went into a branch of C & A and Stella walked out wearing a hat worth twelve pounds for which she had not paid. It was with considerable difficulty that Elsie and Betty forced her to return it.

Once they were home, Stella said, 'I've got to get a drink,' and left the house shouting behind her, 'I'm off to get a man.' She did not reappear for a week.

One night, Bob answered the door to find two policemen standing there with Stella. She had been picked up trying to use an expired train ticket. In due course she was booked for fare evasion and ended up with a criminal record.

Stella kept many of the Kapurthala treasures in Betty's storeroom and in Elsie's loft. During one of her visits, said Elsie,

> ... she stomped around stabbing her high heel shoes through the plaster of my ceiling. My ceiling was a mess but all Stella could do was to abuse me saying it was my fault for having such a poorly built ceiling.

After Stella had worn out her welcome with Betty she was passed on to the eldest sister, Doris. Doris was no match for Stella and after two years she was on the verge of a breakdown. Stella then went to live with Elsie. Elsie had a lodger at the time named Frank. Stella made a play for Frank but was rejected. Stella waited until there was a family gathering to which Frank was invited and then declared, 'Oh everyone knows Elsie and Frank are lovers.' An embarrassed Frank packed his bags that afternoon and Elsie lost her lodger.

Stella then declared she wanted her own home. Elsie took her to meet a number of real estate agents but was mortified when Stella treated them as though they were the lowliest Indian beggars. She demanded a palace for a pittance.

In the late 1960s Stella asked Bob Bishop to go and withdraw money for her from one of her current accounts which held fifty thousand pounds. The same bank held valuables in a safety deposit box. When Bob turned up at the bank he was embarrassed by the tirade the manager delivered for the unpaid service charge on the deposit box dating back several years.

With no Paramjit to pander to her demands, Stella began drinking heavily. Her face became bloated and she wore a scarf tied tightly to hold up her sagging chins. Her red hair came from a bottle and as she was invariably tipsy when she dyed it she ended up with red stains on her forehead and neck. But still she believed she was an attractive young beauty.

Stella was alienating people faster than Elsie could make amends. Elsie had guests for dinner and went down to the local store to buy a bottle of sherry. He told her it was out of stock. 'I'm sorry,' he said. 'That woman in the dark glasses and scarf [referring to Stella] bought it all.'

The doctor was sterner. Stella would constantly call the doctor out to see her. One day she was in his waiting room when he arrived. He looked round the room filled with patients waiting to see him, pointed to Stella and said, 'Right, you. I won't see you for a start.' Stella went back to Elsie's in a fury.

Stella's visits to England bored her. Finally, she stopped going altogether. At first she lived at Delhi's Defence Colony in a modest house but in 1957 she moved into the Annexe of the Hotel Cecil in Simla. Here she met Mr Sethi, who was an employee of the hotel at the time, and they became lovers. Sethi, who was smart and good-looking, was twenty-five and

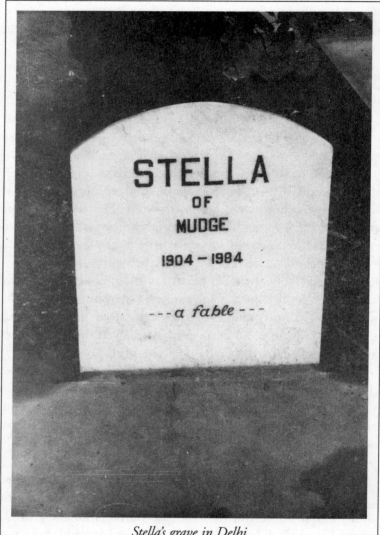

Stella's grave in Delhi

just married; Stella was about sixty. Sethi would 'share' Stella with his friends, and she also had female lovers.

The only people she allowed inside the flat were Sethi and Ram, a hotel employee. The rajah of Jubbal, Stella's step-grandson, recalls seeing Stella pushing her shopping trolley along the Mall in Simla, filled with groceries and bottles of alcohol. He said she was 'not a very nice person. Not a very grandmotherly type'. Around this time she complained to Prince Martand Singh that Sethi had stolen her ironing board and asked him to intervene. Sethi told Martand to 'get lost', so Martand bought Stella a replacement at the market.

Although Stella had set Sethi up in his travel business, he rarely visited her. He put up with her vulgarity for the money he always managed to extract from her. Besides, he had his daughters to think of. Sethi's friend Ajai Singh, who met Stella a number of times, described her as a miser who would sell her beer bottles. Asked what she did during her time in Simla, he said, 'She just drank all the time.' Towards the end, Sethi was looking after her in a manner of speaking, although he wanted to get away. Ajai thinks Stella was holding out on him financially, and it was this that bound him to her, for she held little appeal.

In January 1984 Stella fell in her flat in a drunken stupor and lay unconscious for several days. The police came to break down the door and she was taken to the Simla Sanitarium. She was then transferred to St Stephen's Hospital in Delhi, where she died on 23 February 1984. The only mourners at her simple funeral at the Prithvi Raj Road cemetery were Sethi and an officer from the British high commission.

After Stella's death, Sethi took all her things from her flat, including her jewels, and emptied her bank account. He then left for Canada with one of his three daughters. Stella, maharani of Kapurthala, finally lay at peace under a plain concrete slab.

It was not a tomb fit for a maharani, a police friend told me, after searching the cemetery for her grave. And in death Stella had her final deception. Her tombstone reads 'Estelle Alice Villiers'. In 1999 an anonymous benefactor had a marble headstone erected that reads 'Stella of Mudge "a fable" '.

In 1988 Arcole's of Paris auctioned 157 items of jewellery and other treasures by Boucheron, Cartier, Chaumet, G. Fouquet, Lacloche, Lalique, Marchak and Van Cleef and Arpels, which had once belonged to Stella and which Maharajah Sukhjit had failed to obtain.

The contents of Stella's safety deposit boxes in Swiss banks remain unclaimed. Betty and Elsie visited Switzerland as Stella's next of kin and therefore beneficiaries of her will, but were unable to gain access to the boxes as they did not know the aliases or combinations that Stella had used nor did they have any keys.

In 1997, an English television programme, 'For Love or Money', featured Stella's life story in an attempt to uncover her hidden fortune. The audience was asked, 'Does anyone know where Stella Mudge's treasure is?'

MARGUERITE LAWLER

married Yeshwant Rao Holkar, maharajah of Indore

EUPHEMIA CRANE

married Yeshwant Rao Holkar, maharajah of Indore

*M*arguerite Branyon née Lawler met Yeshwant Rao Holkar, maharajah of Indore, in Los Angeles in 1937. Weakened from drug addiction, alcoholism and chronic insomnia, he weighed a mere thirty-eight kilos and was close to death. He was subject to sudden mood swings and was showing symptoms of manic depressive psychosis although doctors classified it as neurasthenia. Marguerite, who was a nurse-stewardess working for the Union Pacific Railroad, was assigned to look after him and proved such a strength and so devoted that Yeshwant begged her to leave her job and become his full-time nurse and carer. Though she managed to nurse him back to health, she failed to prevent him from sliding back into addiction. Opium poppies grew in abundance on the Malwa plateau in Indore and much of the state's prosperity had been derived from the crop. Yeshwant's dependence on narcotics probably arose from its ready availability.

In 1926 Yeshwant had succeeded his father, Tukoji Rao Holkar, as maharajah. An intelligent but highly strung young man, Yeshwant loved music and the arts. His parents hated each other, maintaining a quarrel of lyric intensity for many years. Tukoji feared that the senior maharani, Yeshwant's mother, described in British documents as 'probably immoral', was a bad influence on the boy. A solitary, inarticulate character, Yeshwant found personal relationships difficult. He was alternately warm and prickly.

In 1923, at the age of fourteen, Yeshwant had been sent to Charterhouse School in England – one of the most highly regarded boys' public schools and a haven of snobbishness and privilege. Discriminated against because of his colour, he hated his time there and made few friends. Yeshwant had been at the school a little over a year when the British forced his father to abdicate and he returned to India and the throne of Indore. He then went to Christ Church, Oxford, where again his natural tendency to be solitary was reinforced by his guardians, the Hardys, who kept potential friends away.

With an annual income of Rs 70,000,000 from the time he became maharajah, Yeshwant displayed a propensity for lavish spending. Abetted by his tutor, he hosted impressive shooting parties which were held at various country houses rented for what British officials considered to be astronomically irresponsible sums. He tried to buy friendship by holding these lavish parties, but without success. As a result of his experiences he developed a lifelong antipathy to the British.

Yeshwant had been fifteen and his first wife, Rani Samyukta Devi, daughter of a junior chief, only eleven when they married in 1924. A daughter, Usha, was born of the union upon whom Yeshwant doted. Once his wife was old enough to leave home, the couple travelled a good deal. The rani developed a preference for America and so Yeshwant built a house there for her and Usha. The rani died in California in 1937, aged only twenty-four.

In April 1938 Marguerite obtained a divorce from her husband Paul Branyon on the grounds of his adultery. Realising that the British would disapprove of him being involved with a divorcee, Yeshwant attempted to hide the fact that Marguerite had been married. He tried, unsuccessfully, to convince them that the name Branyon was an alias, saying that in America women who took up nursing usually adopted an alias, as was done by actresses in England.

In September of that year, in Mexico, Marguerite and Yeshwant were married. Yeshwant described her as 'a lady whom I love from the heart'. In April the following year, ten years after Nancy Miller had married Tukoji, Yeshwant and Marguerite travelled to Indore. They drove to the seven-storeyed Rajwada, the Old Palace, to take darshan, a form of blessing, from the family priest. The Rajwada was a

> monumental stone and wood structure, flanked by bastions and studded with balconies and timber-fronted windows ... testimony to the past grandeur of the Holkars. Its lofty entrance archway above a huge wooden door encrusted with iron studs, lead into a vast courtyard enclosed by galleried rooms, and the arcaded Ganesh Hall.

Yeshwant held a state durbar in the magnificent Ganesh Hall at which he announced that Marguerite was Indore's new maharani. Marguerite addressed the townspeople promising to involve herself in Indore affairs and to attune herself to their problems and concerns. Even the British were impressed. The Resident of Indore described her as 'a sensible, serious lady over thirty, with a genuine desire to use her new position for the benefit of the State and its people'.

Yeshwant owned thirteen magnificent palaces in India, many built in the modernist style by Eckart Muthesius. Unlike many of his fellow princes, he had no wish to have his palaces resemble English country houses. He employed the most avant

garde designers of his day – Le Corbusier, Eileen Gray and
Emile Jacques Ruhlmann – to decorate his main residence in
Indore, the Mani Bagh, and his namesake palace the Yeshwant
Niwas. It was in the Mani Bagh that Yeshwant and Marguerite
set up house.

When deliberating over how much recognition to grant
Marguerite, the British decided that as she was not the guilty
party in her divorce she could meet and mix with Indore's
British community, although not officially. They decided that
the marriage was most definitely morganatic. In official correspondence she was to be styled Maharani Holkar but she was
not to be addressed as Her Highness.

Three months after arriving in Indore Marguerite left
abruptly, complaining that her health had disintegrated. She
explained that she was going to California to seek medical
advice. A combination of Yeshwant's erratic behaviour and the
machinations of the court had worn her down. When the
couple met, it had been Marguerite's robust constitution
and no-nonsense attitude that had attracted Yeshwant. In
Marguerite he found the mother he had never had. At first
the 'mothering' appealed, but the naughty child behaviour it
evoked from him did not appeal to Marguerite. She had
thought Yeshwant would meet her half way and that she
would be the strong right arm that would help him regain an
even keel.

Usha, Yeshwant's daughter from his Indian rani, accompanied Marguerite to the US. She had been five when her
father and Marguerite had married and the two had grown
close. But the people of Indore were unhappy that their little
maharanikumar had gone to live in America.

To provide a safe home for Marguerite and Usha, Yeshwant
built a prison-like residence in Santa Ana, California. It had
heavy concrete walls, bullet-proof glass, steel sashes for its

windows, steel grills for doors, heavy steel bars inside the windows and riflemen's ports at either side of the main door. Yeshwant chose steel as a medium in which to build because heavy charges of electricity could be shot through the grills and sashes by operating a switch in the basement. Built at a cost of fifty thousand dollars, it was a staggering price for what was viewed by the American public as a princely eccentricity.

By 1941 Marguerite's health had improved and she and Usha returned to India, travelling via Sydney. Yeshwant was reported to be eager to have them back. Marguerite found little had changed in Indore during her absence, however, so she and Usha returned to California. Yeshwant would visit them when the mood took him but his visits grew infrequent once he met Euphemia Crane.

When she met Yeshwant Euphemia Crane was married to fellow American Frank Crane, a senior executive at the Hindustan Aircraft Factory in Bangalore. Euphemia was twenty-nine. She had married Frank Crane on 5 July 1936 at the age of twenty-two. Euphemia, or Fay as she was known to friends, lived with her husband and daughter Gwenyth at 6 Crescent Road, Bangalore, a lush tree-lined street in India's garden city. There were other European wives in Bangalore, and there were European clubs, dances and dinner parties, trips to the hill stations and to the luxurious houseboats of Kashmir to keep the expats entertained. Though the circumstances in which they met are unrecorded, by August 1942 Fay and Yeshwant knew each other sufficiently well to go on a trip to Kashmir, with a Mrs McCarty acting as chaperone.

In September they sailed to the US with Fay posing as Yeshwant's secretary, ostensibly to see if Marguerite was receiving proper medical treatment. Being wartime, private travel between India and both Britain and the US was severely curtailed. Berths were scarce, being reserved for emergencies only. Thus Yeshwant's ploy of visiting America to see to Marguerite's health. In fact he went to ask for a divorce. He, Fay and Gwenyth checked into the Carlton Hotel in Washington as Mr and Mrs Holkar and daughter. Frank Crane also colluded in the charade, hoping to avoid publicity to protect Gwenyth. He put it about that Fay had gone to visit her sick mother.

The Resident of Indore, Sir Kenneth Fitze, predicted that Yeshwant and Fay would find Marguerite 'a force with which they will have to reckon', and he was right. When they arrived in California Marguerite was reported to have been 'as mad as a wet hen'.

In order to obtain Marguerite's consent to the divorce, Yeshwant used Usha as a pawn. He promised to give Marguerite custody of the child and a handsome financial settlement if Marguerite agreed to being cited as the guilty party. Thus the divorce plea, which went through uncontested, read that the maharajah was charging Marguerite with 'extreme cruelty' and 'making his life a burden'.

In May 1943 Yeshwant checked into the Palomino Dude Ranch near Reno, Nevada, in order to complete the legal residence requirement prior to seeking his divorce and by July 4 he had completed the required six weeks. Before noon, on July 6, Fay obtained her divorce from Frank Crane on the grounds of 'gross cruelty'. Sir Kenneth Fitze described it 'as obviously a monstrous lie' and commented that 'Hollywood standards had governed recent events'. Fay and Yeshwant were married at 7.30 p.m. that same day.

Though Yeshwant and Fay had sought to keep their divorces and remarriage quiet the story hit the headlines in Washington because the car in which they set out for their honeymoon broke down in Carson City, thirty miles south of Reno. They had to spend the night ignominiously in a glorified garage

Marguerite Lawler

which the press described as a 'honeymoon cottage'. The maharajah had grossly abused his rationing privileges by making a trip of many hundreds of miles. As a result he was formally deprived of his ration book and his driving licence was suspended until the end of September. In one of the many press stories Yeshwant was described as looking the part of a maharajah, with a black moustache and jet black hair and having 'the reputation of being the only man in the world able to plunge his arms up to the elbow in his treasure chests of precious jewels'.

Despite his agreement to allow Usha to stay with Marguerite, Yeshwant took his daughter back to India with him when he and Fay went to Indore later in the year. Marguerite disappeared from official records as she had disappeared from Yeshwant's life.

The British were appalled at the stories in the press and retribution was swift. Yeshwant was described as 'a lounge lizard and a liar'. In October 1943 it was recorded by the British:

> Nor should it be forgotten that this Prince, behind a smoke screen of lies; neurasthenia; precarious health, and all the rest of it, has seduced another man's wife in circumstances that would preclude for life any Englishman who had so behaved from the presence of the Sovereign!

In October 1944, F. Wylie, secretary to the political department, explained Britain's attitude towards Fay in a conversation with the maharajah of Dewas (Senior):

> I was more than sorry that this incident had arisen but after all it was not me but His Highness Holkar

who had run away with another man's wife and married her incontinently in Hollywood or some such exotic place. The man was a Prince whether he liked it or not and noblesse oblige. The English people had thrown out a King Emperor for conduct of that sort. Was it surprising that this lady, after all her adventurous experiences in the matrimonial field, was not allowed straightaway to occupy one of the seniormost places among the matrons of India viz., as the consort of the Maharaja Holkar?

Yeshwant apologized for his conduct but the authorities were unmoved. Though Fay was described by the British as 'socially better than Marguerite' and was considered quiet, charming, an attentive hostess, domestically-minded and devoted to her husband, the couple had not only transgressed racially and socially, but also morally.

The British declared that Fay was not to bear the title Maharani Holkar. She

> ... was not to be treated as a respectable member of society on the same basis as ladies of unblemished reputation such as Pudukkottai and Palanpur in view of the fact she had travelled to America with the Maharajah and stayed with him in a hotel.

Yeshwant did have a small victory, however. Soon after he and Fay were married they had presented themselves at the British consulate in Los Angeles and Fay had been issued with a passport in the name of Maharani Holkar.

Perhaps Fay thought she would be able to turn Yeshwant away from the bad habits which were already obvious at the time she married him. Once they had settled in Indore, however, the relationship went rapidly downhill. Yeshwant's prime minister Dina Nath became Fay's implacable enemy, which added to her troubles. He blamed her for dragging Yeshwant into an international scandal by encouraging him to send, in 1942, an open letter to President Roosevelt urging the intervention by the courts of the US, China and Russia to settle the differences between India and Britain. The British were furious and in the ensuing scandal Yeshwant was almost forced to abdicate. He clung on, to have Fay then accused by Dina Nath of being the associate of gangsters and a drug addict who had only married the maharajah to get her hands on the Holkar jewellery. He also blamed her for Yeshwant's increasing addiction to morphine. Nath was duly sacked by Yeshwant, but the situation improved little.

Though Fay, like Marguerite before her, had promised to involve herself in Indore's affairs, she had her hands full dealing with Yeshwant whose addictions were causing him to behave in an increasingly erratic way. He slept all day, not bothering to change out of his night clothes. Always thin, he became positively emaciated and was a bundle of nerves. The British warned their women not to leave their visiting cards at the palace and to stay away from any function attended by the maharajah. Events came to a head when he outraged British women guests at his own New Year's Party by appearing in his pyjamas. His aide-de-camp explained to British officials that Yeshwant's addiction to narcotics was at the heart of the matter.

The Resident of Indore had observed at the time of Fay and Yeshwant's marriage that Fay was a more up-to-date woman than one would normally encounter in Britain, but she had little outlet in Indore for her unconventionality. Besides, the birth of her son Richard in 1944 caused her to seek stability. Yeshwant was not an appropriate role model. Fay complained bitterly to Nancy Miller that 'she was fed up with him and did not want her baby son brought up in this atmosphere'. Though Nancy commiserated, there was little she could do, for she could not appear to be taking sides against her own stepson and Indore's maharajah.

Fay saw there was little chance of her ever being accepted by the British community as a woman of good standing. She continued to be unable to appear as maharani at any gatherings in Indore attended by British officials and their wives. Knowing that the British disapproved of her no more than they did her husband was particularly humiliating. Even with independence looming, matters did not change. In November 1946 King George VI was reprimanded by the India Office for referring to Fay as maharani in a telegram he and the queen had sent thanking the Holkars for their good wishes.

Nine months later Yeshwant had a revenge of sorts when the princes were to sign the Instrument of Accession handing their states over to India and Pakistan. Yeshwant was one of the few princes who held out against merging with independent India. Viceroy Mountbatten was adamant that independence could only work if all the princes merged with either of the two countries. Yeshwant signed the Instrument only at the very last moment, then sent it to Mountbatten by ordinary post.

Disillusioned with life in India and troubled by her increasingly erratic husband, upon independence in August 1947 Fay headed back to California, taking Richard with her. Fay and Yeshwant's marriage had foundered on his drug addiction and his general instability. Whether this instability resulted from the eccentric streak that was said to run through the Holkar family or whether it came from his drug use it is difficult to say.

From the time of their marriage Fay and Yeshwant had been frequent visitors to the US and when Fay made her home in

California Yeshwant commuted back and forth between India and the US. Yeshwant was fond of Americans and they appreciated his liberal views and anti-imperialist sentiments. So rarely was he seen in his principality that the Resident of Indore suggested that the state anthem should be 'Some Day My Prince Will Come' — a well-known song from the movie *Snow White and the Seven Dwarfs.*

Fay and Yeshwant were divorced in 1960 and in December 1961 Yeshwant died of cancer at Breach Candy Hospital in Bombay.

Richard Holkar was never recognized as his father's heir. Like his grandfather and father before him, he married an American – a woman he met while they were fellow students of political science at Stanford University. For some years Richard and Sally Holkar enjoyed a jet-set existence but in due course they made their principal residence in Bombay's sophisticated waterside suburb of Worli. Richard became a jeweller and Sally involved herself in journalism and writing Indian cookbooks. The two of them also set up a successful weaving centre, the Rehwa Society, situated in Maheshwar on the Narmada River, two hours' drive from Indore. Here they nurtured the dying art of Maheshwar weaving, turning it into a thriving business run as a co-operative by the women weavers themselves.

Usha, upon whom the state of Indore was bestowed by order of the British, with their usual distaste for mixed-race heirs, lives in Bombay's old-established suburb of Colaba not far from Joan Palanpur's stepson, Nawab Taley Khan.

Lady Fay Holkar lives in Santa Rosa, California.

JOAN FALKINER

married Nawab Taley Mohamed Khan of Palanpur

As *The Melbourne Truth* noted, Joan Falkiner was 'born with her teeth clenched on the proverbial silver spoon'. Her paternal grandfather, Franc Sadleir Falkiner, had emigrated to Australia from Tipperary, Ireland. He married Emily Elizabeth Bazley and they produced nine children, the youngest of whom was Leigh, born in 1880. By the time of his death in 1909, Franc Falkiner owned a number of rural properties and had become a prosperous man. By this time the Falkiner family was selling rams all over the world, particularly in New Zealand and South Africa.

In 1901 Leigh Falkiner was made company secretary of his family's holdings and in 1910 he became manager of Wanganella Estate. Leigh and his brother Otway went into partnership and were extremely successful.

In 1939, apart from his pastoral interests, Leigh owned a house in Melbourne's Domain Road, South Yarra, a house at Mount Macedon and a villa in Cannes.

Leigh and his wife Beatrice had three children: Ann, Joan and Leigh Junior. The family was well-travelled, and they spent several years in England and Europe. They attended the coronation of King George VI and like other wealthy people of the time, they spent time relaxing and taking the waters at a number of Europe's health resorts.

Joan was an extrovert and had many friends. She also had no shortage of admirers, given her good looks, her social position and her amiable personality. She was welcome in the homes not only of the most respectable Australian families but also those of England and Europe. There was a side to Joan that yearned for the unconventional, for something that differed from the expectations of those around her. It is interesting that *The Melbourne Truth* made comparisons between her and Molly Fink. Not only were there the obvious similarities – both women being beautiful Melbournians with good connections – but both of them were also risk takers.

In 1937 Joan was holidaying with her family at Freiburg in Germany, taking the cure. Also at Freiburg was Nawab Taley Khan of Palanpur who had been a regular visitor to the spa since he had injured his spine in a riding accident. He and his son, Iqbal, had just been to London to attend the coronation of George VI. Iqbal, who was about Joan's age, introduced her to his father and once she had become acquainted with the confident, urbane Taley, she paid little attention to his son.

Like so many Indian princes, Taley spent much of his time travelling. Taley's wife never accompanied him on his trips overseas. As a strict Muslim it would have been difficult for her to keep the purdah she was accustomed to in India. She was also in poor health and preferred to spend her time in prayer and meditation. Though she had given him a son, and he had profound respect for her, she was not a companion who could share in his wider world.

Joan was hauntingly beautiful and exactly the companion Taley had been hoping to find. For several years he had been asking his friend Prince Mohamed of Egypt to keep an eye out for a suitable second wife. The British had been alerted to his search and had told him that he should focus his attention on women of Oriental origin, but Taley had other intentions.

Joan was equally attracted to Taley but she was underage and would have had to obtain her parents' permission to marry. She knew they would not agree to her marrying an Indian, whatever his status. The lovers therefore decided to bide their time and keep their romance a secret.

Palanpur (now part of Gujarat) was a small state of eighteen hundred square miles with a population of 315,000. The region is mostly sandy plains, liable to drought, with small pockets of jungle. Palanpur state was established in the sixteenth century but its origins stretched back to the twelfth century when Afghani tribesmen swept down into Marwar and took possession of 360 townships. Until Independence, the nawabs of Palanpur held their title as diwan, bestowed by Emperor Akbar, as their most esteemed honorific.

Taley Mohamed Khan was born in 1892, joined the Imperial Cadet Corps in 1903, married the daughter of a Muslim ruler of an adjacent state in 1906, and succeeded to the gaddi in 1918. His father had had him educated in Palanpur, where he learnt the languages of his subjects as well as the courtly language of the Mughal-Persians. He learned how to rule the state, and how to manage his advisers and prime minister so as not to be in 'the pocket' of any particular faction, noted the political agent with some satisfaction. The agent reported that Taley was dignified, accessible, popular, and played no favourites. The welfare of his subjects was paramount. He built new hospitals and encouraged industrialization and the use of irrigation. During his rule Palanpur became almost self-sufficient in the production of food grains.

Taley was popular with the British. He gave Britain financial support during the First World War although he was not eligible for active service because of his injured spine. In 1920 he was made a Knight Commander of the Indian Empire and he headed the Chamber of Princes in 1920 and 1921. He was

*Nawab Taley Khan of Palanpur with Iqbal Khan (left),
his son from his first wife, and nephew*

aide-de-camp to young Prince Edward during his 1921 tour of India and honorary aide-de-camp to George VI in 1937. In 1922 he was awarded the KCVO and in 1932 the GCIE. In 1936 he was made an honorary colonel and in 1928 he was a member of the Indian deputation to the League of Nations.

When Joan turned twenty-one, she announced her intention to marry Taley. As the press noted, the news landed like a grenade among Melbourne's society. Sections of the press lauded her decision to go against the mores of society to marry the man she loved. Certainly it took courage, for she knew the social ostracism she was going to have to face. Joan was not simply infatuated with Taley; she had proved the strength of her feelings by waiting several years to marry him. Leigh Falkiner thought that while Taley was a good chap to have a yarn with, he was most definitely not the sort of husband white people of breeding would want for their daughters.

Taley wanted Joan to be well aware of the difficulties of becoming his wife. He had explained the impediments carefully: he was Muslim, he was black, he was already married with two grown-up children, he was thirty years her senior and not in good health. She would have to be in purdah when in Palanpur. But Joan brushed all this aside:

Joan and Taley were married in a quiet ceremony in Taley's private quarters in the Zora Mahal Palace. Joan converted to Islam and took on a Muslim name, becoming Begum Jahanara.

Practially everyone except the couple themselves was dismayed by the union. The British were aghast. The India Office mandarins scurried around searching for intelligence about Joan's background. The Australian high commissioner in London assured them that 'Miss Falkiner is of good social position, antecedents, and character'. But such assurances were not enough. The India Office decided that formal recognition of Joan was out of the question. The only concession that they would make was that the Residents for Rajputana and the Western Rajputana states could meet and entertain her at informal dinners.

Before their marriage, Taley had tried to win the British over by promising that he would never seek Joan's recognition nor the rights of any children they might have to the succession. Taley had promised they would live a quiet and dignified life away from the public eye.

Understandably, Taley's wife was unhappy at the marriage. She envied Joan and her sister Ann their freedom to go where they wished and do what they liked. She told Ann that all she had ever learned to do was to cook sweetmeats. As an aristocratic Muslim she had been brought up in strict purdah with the express purpose of marrying, producing children and thereby accomplishing her life's purpose. Iqbal had not been a strong child and on a number of occasions his parents had feared he would die. His mother fussed over him and made him, more than his older sister, the purpose of her life. She lived her life vicariously through Iqbal, knowing one day it would be the flesh of her flesh who would rule Palanpur.

Taley and Joan went to Kashmir for their honeymoon. There Joan received a cable from her Aunt Una trying to dissuade her from marriage. Joan cabled back: 'Many thanks your cable and kindly interest already married and extremely happy staying fortnight with His Highness Kashmir Writing Love Joan Begum Palanpur.'

Though Taley's annual income of eighty-two thousand pounds was modest by princely standards, he maintained a city palace, the Zora Mahal, for which the finest craftsmen of Palanpur were employed to do the decorative interior wood-work. There were magnificent frescoes on the ceiling of the durbar hall and the intricate plasterwork was gilded in places to contrast with the darker shades of green and peacock blue. Joan and Taley had their own suite of rooms separate from the children. They had their personal chefs and food tasters as well as their personal servants. In all, there were 125 servants at the palace. Iqbal remembers that early in her marriage Joan had an Australian companion but she later engaged a French lady's maid.

Twelve kilometers outside Palanpur, at Balaram on the Mount Abu Road, Taley had his country palace. It lay at the edge of the jungle which was home to leopard, deer, bear, peacock and the occasional tiger. Today, restored to its former glory, with marble fountains and manicured gardens, the palace is a luxury hotel.

In the cool of Mount Abu, Joan and Taley had a hot weather residence that looked across the Nakki Lake. Mount Abu in Rajasthan was a favoured hill station for the rulers of Rajasthan and Gujarat. It was here that Joan entertained many of their European friends. They also had a house in Breach Candy in Bombay, which Taley had bought for Joan. Abroad, they had a house in the south of France where Joan's parents also had a fine residence.

From October to March Joan and Taley lived in Palanpur. From April to September they stayed in Abu and Bombay. In April, when Palanpur began to heat up, they moved to Bombay. Sometimes they visited Mussoorie to join in the social life with other princes and their European wives.

Visits to the Breach Candy house involved detailed preparations, with elaborate wardrobes having to be prepared for Joan and Taley's lively social life. Large numbers of Europeans lived in Bombay, especially during the war years, and life was a whirl of activity.

Joan chose to wear saris when in India, preferring chiffon, which she found particularly flattering. In Europe, however,

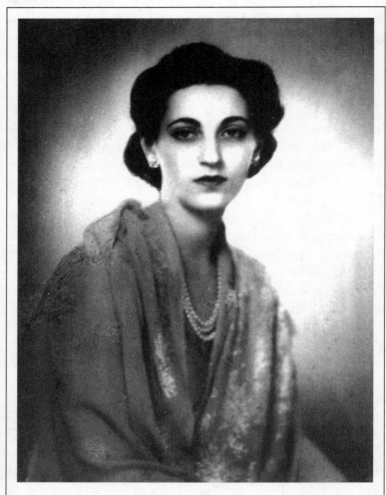

Joan Falkiner

she wore them only occasionally in the evening. Yuvraj Digvijay Sinh of Wankaner says that Joan was one of the most beautiful women he had ever seen. 'She had sharp features and a beautiful smile. Her beauty was haunting.'

Palanpur was renowned for its diamonds and Taley had given Joan a magnificent diamond solitaire engagement ring. (Joan sent home diamonds of almost equal quality to her mother and sister in Australia. When they wore them to a ball in Melbourne, an acquaintance came up and enquired of Beatrice, 'Oh, are they from the nawab's vaults?' Beatrice was so miffed she never wore Joan's diamonds again.)

For Joan, as for the other European wives of Muslim princes, life at home was more sequestered than it was for white women married to Hindus. A Muslim wife, especially an aristocratic one, was generally expected to keep strict purdah. While Joan managed to escape the confinement of traditional purdah, she could never simply walk down the streets of Palanpur and investigate its higgledy-piggledy shops. Even an average memsahib of the Raj, constrained by her own self-imposed apartheid, enjoyed more freedom than the European wives of princes. It is partly because of this that many of them spent so much of their time in Europe.

Upon waking Joan would dress and then share an informal breakfast with Taley. They then went their separate ways: Taley to attend to official business and to hold durbars, public audiences for those subjects who sought his advice or his intervention in family squabbles and issues regarding land. Joan had her correspondence to attend to; she would regularly visit the state's hospitals and schools; and she had visitors to entertain. Among the couple's many friends were princes such as the maharajahs of Bikaner, Jodhpur, Kapurthala, Patiala, Kashmir and Prince Mohamed of Egypt. They also had numerous high-ranking British friends, such as the Mountbattens.

Joan's days were always busy. She kept a strict eye on the running of the family's many residences, and over the years saw to their redecoration. Given their extensive social life, she was also kept busy seeing to the million and one details that ensured their guests' comfort and entertainment. For relaxation she rode and hunted. After her daughter Shameem's birth in 1943, Joan had her upbringing and subsequent studies to supervise.

By princely standards, however, Joan and Taley led a relatively quiet life. Taley sought Joan's advice about Palanpur's modernization, irrigation and industrialization. He was keen to have her by his side when British officials visited as she made such a good impression. Official correspondence, often harsh in its observations of the princely states, especially when their ranis were white women, spoke of Joan in glowing terms as being 'an asset rather than a liability'.

Joan often told her family in her letters how contented she was with her life in Palanpur. This was particularly the case in her correspondence with her Aunt Una, who saw herself as something of an intermediary between Joan and her parents. Joan wrote to her aunt in April 1940 that,

> I have not had time to find Palanpur dull, yet, and I feel that I never will. I like it very much, and always feel glad to be back after our trips. I felt rather more like a visitor for the first two or three months, but now I feel quite at home.

For a long time after her marriage Joan was happy to remain in India. She was well aware that the Indian princes' frequent and prolonged visits abroad caused friction between them and their British rulers. The British, for their part, realized that despite frequent maladministration, the squandering of state incomes, the eccentricities, and sometimes pronounced cruelty and neglect, the princely states were less prone to rebellion and civil unrest than the British-administered parts of India. Hoary traditions and reciprocal relations provided civil stability. Even notoriously cruel princes such as the maharajah of Alwar and Bhupinder Singh of Patiala were mourned by hundreds of thousands of their oppressed subjects upon their deaths. And so Joan's willingness to support Taley in Palanpur and to remain in India was much appreciated by India's political administration.

In due course, however, the Palanpurs came to regularly visit the south of France so that they could spend time with Joan's parents, her sister Ann and Ann's family. Little Shameem revelled in Cannes' easy familiarity. She loved the azure water, her pets, the parties she shared with cousins and the doting grandfather who reminded her much of her own father. Her grandmother had reservations, however. Shameem was not the grandchild Beatrice had hoped for. But despite Beatrice's standoffishness the summers passed pleasantly and in Cannes Joan and Taley could be convinced that all was right with the world.

It was in Cannes, at the Hotel Provencale, that Joan and Taley were informed, just two days before Independence, that Joan had finally been recognized by the British government. As of 13 August 1947 she was to be addressed as Her Highness the Begum of Palanpur. This recognition of Taley's dedication and loyalty had come too late. The kingdom over which Joan could now preside as Her Highness was wiped out at midnight of August 14 when Jawaharlal Nehru ushered in the Indian nation.

Independence finally spurred Taley to leave India. While he still ruled Palanpur he was prepared to stay in India for most of the year even though the heat was not good for his health, or for Joan's. His responsibilities to his people took precedence. Following Independence, however, he decided that he and Joan would spend at least half the year in Egypt. Egypt's Prince Mohamed Ali welcomed many of Europe's and India's erstwhile rulers. The climate was pleasant and Europe's old ruling elite and India's princes could continue to employ an army of retainers, as they had in earlier times.

From 1950 to 1953 Joan and Taley spent six months of the year in their house in Cannes and six months in Cairo. By 1954, however, Taley was becoming too infirm to even make the journey to Cairo.

During 1954 Taley's first wife died, and this was a source of grief to him. She could not have been faulted in the devotion she had showed to their children nor to the god they had in common. Taley was well aware that Joan's conversion to Islam had been to please him and to satisfy his family traditions. But Iqbal's mother had woven Islam into the very fabric of her being. Her death opened old wounds for Taley and left him feeling guilty.

Joan and Taley spent an increasing amount of time at their house in Mount Abu. The view out over the lake was soothing to Taley's spirit. He had become bitter and disillusioned after the integration of the princely states into the Indian Union. He felt something better could have been done for the princes. He knew that he could rely on Iqbal to manage his financial affairs but he was worried about what was to become of Joan and Shameem. Shameem was still a child and her marriage had not yet been negotiated.

In recent times Taley's family had taken spouses from the nearby state of Dasada. His own first wife was the daughter of Malek Shri Rustam Khanji of Dasada, a Pathan like the Palanpurs. Iqbal, too, had married into the Dasada family. In earlier times the Palanpur nawabs had married Rajput wives – the finest Hindu royalty. But what traditional Muslim would marry his daughter, a girl of mixed race whose mother was not an orthodox Muslim? Taley feared that when he was gone Iqbal would not have his father's commitment to finding Shameem a suitable husband. And Joan, though he loved her dearly, could not be expected to understand the customs and traditions that drove a Muslim prince.

By 1957, the illness that had been causing Taley considerable pain and discomfort was diagnosed as cancer. At the house at Mount Abu he lay on the terrace and looked out over the still waters of the lake where the wooden boats went back and forth. As the end drew near Taley became alternately agitated and then quiet. Joan stayed by his side constantly and Iqbal was there to do his father's bidding and listen to any last-minute instructions.

Comatose, Taley finally exhaled his last. Joan wept. Shameem was too young to fully take in the enormity of her loss. Iqbal knew he had to be strong and clearheaded for, as was the Muslim way, he had to take control after his father's death.

Taley's body was brought down by the morning train from Abu. As the news spread through Palanpur, the town's populace wept. Taley had been their mai-baap, their mother and father, for as long as most people could remember. He had been a sincere and devoted ruler. He had ensured that the transition from princely state to Independent India had gone smoothly and his compliance had resulted in there being little Muslim-Hindu violence in Palanpur.

Iqbal headed the male mourners who accompanied the body out to the burial ground. Joan, as was the custom, remained at the palace with her head covered by a shawl.

After the funeral, Iqbal stayed on in Palanpur to tidy up his father's affairs. Soon there was conflict between him and Joan over her allowance. Joan had been accustomed to managing her own affairs and Taley had never questioned her requirements. She began to feel financially constrained. To make matters worse, her father, thinking 'old Palanpur', as he called him, had plenty of money and would take care of Joan's future, had left Joan little in his will.

Joan stayed on in India until 1957, hoping to be able to make a life for herself. It was, after all, Shameem's home. She also spent a considerable amount of time in France and England. In 1960, feeling frustrated by Iqbal's control over her financial affairs and therefore, to some degree, her movements, Joan returned to Australia to seek her mother's advice.

She and Shameem gave an interview to the *Australian Women's Weekly*. Shameem told reporters she was not used to attending unchaperoned parties. She said that in India girls went out in groups, which is what she preferred, rather than alone with a boyfriend. She also said she preferred wearing a sari to Western dress, finding it much more comfortable.

Shameem had been in England at Heathfield School, and was to go on to Stafford House. Then, she said, she wanted to study science at an English or European university. Her ambition was to be a scientist. She was not interested in being a social butterfly, or being a star debutante at London parties.

In the interview Shameem came across as a serious, modest and unaffected young woman who was in tune with her Indian background. At about this time she told the maharajah of Drangadhra that she wanted to be a doctor and practice in Palanpur. In the years that followed, however, Shameem seems to have had increasing difficulty with her circumstances. In time she joined a Buddhist monastery and disappeared from sight. Even her mother was unaware of her whereabouts.

Joan went to live in the south of France where she soon had a number of male admirers. Like Molly Fink before her, however, she was unwilling to remarry and give up her title.

*Princess Shameem (left), daughter of Nawab Taley Khan,
with her cousin*

Joan began drinking heavily and her face showed the tight perfection achieved by the surgeon's knife. The alchohol made her vague and she became somewhat cut off from the world. Shameem continued to live incognito: even Iqbal, who was eager to get her to sign some papers, was unable to find her.

In 1991 Joan was still living in the south of France but was too vague and forgetful to take proper care of herself. By 1999 she had moved into a nursing home in Australia at Noosa Heads. Despite being more than eighty she was still conscious of her looks and her appeal to men.

By 1999 Iqbal had sold the house in Abu, the Zora Mahal Palace and the palace at Balaram. All that remains of his patrimony is a small house in the grounds of the City Palace.

Taley is buried in a marble grave beside his first wife. Over the graves is a simple shed-like structure and pigeons fly in and out. The building is in stark contrast to the magnificent marble and sandstone mausoleums built over the graves of his ancestors, but these are now in a sorry state, having been pulled apart by looters.

SANDRA McBRYDE

married Hanwant Singh, maharajah of Jodhpur

*T*he desert kingdom of Jodhpur, or Marwar as it is known in Rajput lore, was founded in 1459 by Rao Jodha. It covered an area of thirty-five thousand square miles, equal in size to Ireland. Rao Jodha fathered twelve sons who he hoped would keep his kingdom safe against Mughal depredation.

Maharajah Hanwant Singh, a direct descendant of Rao Jodha, was one of the richest men in the world. In 1930, it was calculated that his father, Umaid Singh, maharajah of Jodhpur, owned between two and three million pounds' worth of jewels alone. Rosita Forbes describes the treasures:

> There were children's toys of solid gold, nursery balls set with rubies, rosewater basins, dishes, jugs, perfume bottles, censers, betel-nut sets and palm-leaf boxes all made of gold. There were writing table sets encrusted with precious stones, swords whose scabbards and hilts were of emeralds, diamonds and pearls. There was gold- and silver-plated furniture, women's shoes sewn with diamonds, an expanding cap made of the finest solitaire diamonds, eyebrows of diamonds with hooks to hold them over the ears and enamelled crutches for the infirm, their handles studded with gems.

The family that gave its name to riding breeches were patrons of the fledgling Indian airline industry as well as consummate horsemen. Umaid had an airfield constructed near Jodhpur city where a flying club was established, run by a British pilot.

Hanwant, the eldest of Umaid's five sons, was born in 1923. He married his first wife, an Indian, in 1943, when she was seventeen. In 1947 he succeeded his father as the twenty-fourth Rathore ruler of Jodhpur – the Rathores being a warrior caste reputedly descended from the moon. Hanwant was an unusually talented man of eclectic skills. He was an enthusiastic magician and earned membership of the Magic Circle Club through his consummate performance with fire and rabbits in front of six hundred wizards and their friends.

Sandra McBryde was working as matron in a Bombay nursing home when she met Hanwant at a party. He invited her to Jodhpur and soon she was installed in the massive Umaid Bhavan Palace as his mistress. The palace, the construction of which was begun in 1927 by Umaid Singh, was so large that it could easily accommodate Hanwant's first wife as well as Sandra without their ever having to meet. (Hanwant also had a magnificent house, Aranmore, in Ooty, built and furnished along Scottish baronial lines.)

There is some confusion as to whether Sandra was in fact an Anglo-Indian, rather than Scottish as some reports suggest. In a letter to his son 'Bubbles' Bhawani Singh, Maharajah Jai Singh of Jaipur wrote angrily,

> ... your cousin is not only financially broke, but ... has made history by marrying a common Eurasian girl and has lowered himself and his State in the eyes of the public.

In desert country, the state of Jodphur was distinguished by its majestic Meherangarh Fort – the finest fort in 'fort-studded Rajasthan'. One can well imagine Sandra's thoughts when she passed through the three gates of her husband's fort for the first time. First there was the Jayapol Gate, scarred by the cannon balls of successive invaders, then the Fatehpol, the Victory Gate, and finally the Lahapol Gate. Beside the Lahapol Gate were the childlike handprints of Maharajah Man Singh's fifteen widows who, upon his death in 1843, committed sati.

Of the zenana, journalist Gayatri Sinha writes that it was built

> in honeycomb fashion with rooms leading into each other, with exquisite jali worked windows and bangalas overlooking a central courtyard. It must have once housed a small army of wives. On rare occasions the wives would accompany the maharajah on hunts or festival occasions but remained for most part within purdah in the zenana dodhi. These once elegant quarters are now bat and pigeon infested and await the next phase of restoration at the fort!

In September 1948 Sandra and Hanwant were married according to Arya Samaj rites, and Sandra took the name Sundra Devi. Sandra was only nineteen when she persuaded the maharajah to marry her – she was sufficiently worldly wise to realize that marriage would give her greater security than being his mistress. It was that same year that Hanwant's Indian wife gave birth to Gaj Singh, the maharajah's heir.

Maharani Sandra wore heavy silk saris embroidered with jewels. Even her jackets were stitched with the finest of Jodhpur gems. On one occasion, travelling to England from India, Sandra and Hanwant's ship docked at Tilbury. The two of them had one of the furious rows for which their relationship was noted. In a temper tantrum, Sandra threw her diamond-studded jacket overboard. Ann Morrow writes,

> She refused to come ashore at Tilbury. She stayed
> in her cabin dressed in her gold sari and twiddling
> her Indian bangles and for five hours the panto-
> mime went on. Eventually a couple of hefty dockers
> jumped in the water and retrieved the jacket and
> later felt the warm touch of a gold sovereign in their
> palms.

In 1949 Sandra and Hanwant came to London and stayed at the Claridges. They had come to visit her family and to attend the christening of her nephew, Keith McBryde. Her brother, who was a travelling salesman, lived in Stoke-on-Trent.

Sandra found that her position as a second wife gave her little authority within the palace household and the brooding animosity towards her exhibited by the staff was palpable. She knew well the dangers she faced as a firangi woman who had 'stolen' the maharajah away from his rightful wife and son.

In 1952, returning from a successful election campaign for the Lok Sabha in which he stood as an Independent, Hanwant's plane crashed into telegraph wires, killing him instantly. When voting was finalized it was found that he had won his seat by ten thousand votes.

Sandra was only twenty-three when Hanwant was killed. She knew the zenana women hated her. Gaj Singh, who was only four years old, would be maharajah one day and he had no reason to like the woman who had usurped the status of his beloved and aristocratic mother. Sandra was an affront to Rajput pride. The people only wanted to think fine thoughts of their late maharajah and her presence in Jodhpur was deeply resented.

Sandra believed herself fortunate to have escaped with her life after her husband's death. Some years later, she told her nephew Keith of palace retainers making veiled threats and of women being bricked up alive inside the zenana. Certainly it was a tradition in Jodhpur for the wives of deceased maharajahs to kill themselves by committing sati – throwing themselves onto their husbands' funeral pyres. Though no European wife ever committed sati, as recently as 1911 the seventy-four wives of Jodhpur's Maharajah Sardar Singh threw themselves on the funeral pyre. Charles Allen writes, 'Nowhere in Rajasthan were satis more honoured by memorials and by worship than in Jodhpur.' He tells the story of the last royal sati which took place in Jodhpur in the 1950s. A month before her husband died, the sati, Sugankunverba, stopped eating and drinking. As soon as her husband breathed his last she began her preparations. She bathed and put on wedding finery: ivory bangles, her jewels, the wives' red sindoor, and a pink silk chiffon sari embroidered with gold zari. She accompanied her husband's body to the burning ghat and there sat with him as the fires lapped high around them. She chanted 'Ram-Ram' until the voice died within her and then she and her husband's charred bones were picked out and taken and immersed in the Ganges at Hardwar.

Sandra left Jodhpur without delay, returning to England where she took up nursing once again. She never remarried. Certainly, it would have been hard for her to find a man who could match Hanwant. She spent the remainder of her professional life nursing and died of cancer at the age of sixty-two.

YVONNE MARTIN

married Nawabzada Mohamed Mubarak Abbasi
of Bahawalpur

*E*stelle Stone met Yvonne Abbasi in a dress shop in Sydney, where Yvonne was working as a sales assistant. Yvonne was tiny, with long dark hair, alabaster skin and beautiful blue eyes. The two women became acquainted and started going to parties together.

Yvonne told Estelle that she had left her husband behind in Pakistan. He was a Muslim prince, she said – Nawabzada Mohamed Abbasi of Bahawalpur, nicknamed Riki. She had run away from her husband's palace in Pakistan, fearing for her life. She had left her four young sons behind, along with the Rolls Royces, the jewels and the servants. 'What use are they to me if I'm dead?' she said.

Yvonne's story was the stuff of nightmares. 'She was mixed up,' said Estelle. 'I visited her in the mental hospital. I really feel they must have done something to her mind over there in Pakistan.'

Yvonne told Estelle she'd met Riki while working as a secretary in the Pakistani consulate in Sydney. She fell in love with his dark good looks and they married in 1952. All went well until they returned to Pakistan, to Riki's kingdom in the desert, where his father, the nawab, was ruler. Yvonne complained of the machinations of the nawab's wives and concubines, locked away in the harem where they had nothing better to do than plot and conspire against the firangi woman who had captured young Prince Riki's heart, as other unwelcome white women, long ago, had ensnared the nawab's heart.

In *Beyond Belief,* V.S. Naipaul writes of a journey he made out into the desert wasteland of Bahawalpur, an erstwhile state whose origins lay in old Baghdad. Yvonne's father-in-law, the old nawab of Bahawalpur, or 'Brownie' as they called him at school in England, is the stuff of which myths are made. He gave no thought whatsoever to administration nor to the welfare of his subjects. He did not see his rule as a relationship of reciprocity with his people or view it as a sacred trust. He was simply a plunderer.

The nawab was made an honorary captain in the Indian Army and appointed aide-de-camp to the Prince of Wales during his 1922 tour of India, but he was considered to be of unstable temperament, poor heredity and weak, though he was an amiable and lavish host at his London residence.

In his harem the nawab had once had as many as 390 women, and Riki's mother, Linda Sayce, had been one of the nawab's three English wives. According to V.S. Naipaul, the nawab conceived of white women as imperial trophies. In accordance with custom, Prince Riki was, after his mother's death, raised in the harem until he was five.

Though the British authorities had been alerted to sinister activities in the nawab's harem, they had turned a blind eye. Inconveniently, they received a letter from Gladys Bishop, Linda Sayce's sister in Bombay, making accusations against the nawab.

According to Gladys, following Linda's death her daughter Therese had been sent away to the convent of Jesus and Mary in Simla and her two sons, princes David and Riki, were being kept in a hidden armoury in Bahawalpur Palace. Gladys had

The old nawab of Bahawalpur with his English wife Linda Sayce

been unable to obtain a death certificate for Linda and feared that she had been murdered.

The British advocated the destruction of Gladys' letter. If a scandal involving a European woman came to light it would need to be investigated and anything involving the nawab of Bahawalpur would be like opening a can of worms.

It was not only the British who wished to hide the unsavoury goings-on in the Bahawalpur palace. Naipaul writes that after Independence when the Pakistani army took over the palace,

> ... they found a whole collection of dildos. About 600, some made of clay, some bought in England and battery operated. The army dug a pit and buried these dildos. A lot of dirty magazines. He needed them to use the dildos. He became impotent very early. His appetites were sated.

Naipaul suggests that the nawab's appeal to European and Eastern women alike lay in his wealth,

> After his foreign trips, he [the nawab] would enter the harem with tin trunks and the women would go crazy. They had asked for chemise and chiffons and feathers and they would fight for these things. For the English wives, he would shop at Tiffany's, Cartier, Garrard. The salesmen would come to him when he was in England and show the jewels. For himself he bought English country scenes and he always had English portrait painters come to paint him.

Unable to attract white women from the upper classes, the nawab had nevertheless become sufficiently rich through the

Sutlej Valley Project that irrigated his desert to obtain white women from what the British referred to as the bottom drawer. Apparently the nawab's last English wife was known locally as Lady O because British officials and the Bahawalpur gentry judged her to be common.

In *Highness*, Ann Morrow writes of the curious circumstances in which the nawab obtained another of his 'common' English wives.

> ... he was having freshly squeezed orange juice in his hotel suite in London and reading the newspaper when he saw the equivalent of a stunning page 3 girl. But in those days it was a beauty queen, Katherine Scott, aged sixteen, and fully clothed. She had just been to the J. Arthur Rank charm school and won a screen test with Ray Milland. The Prince rushed out, ordered every rose in the florist's and proposed to this railway porter's daughter from London; they were married three weeks later at Caxton Hall. 'I didn't know he was a Prince,' she said innocently. Her father said he could not go to the wedding because he could not afford to lose a day's pay.

The nawab had separate quarters for his European and Indian wives. A journalist from Bahawalpur who had come to know one of the women of the nawab's harem told Naipaul how

> In the palace, he had a separate building for the English wives and their children. The Indian wives knew about the English wives but the English women never knew about the Indian wives. When he wanted

to go to the harem, he would say he was going on tour. Sometimes he would be there for three days, sometimes a week. And there would be a proper escort; the guards, the Rolls Royce, the Camel Corps who were his personal bodyguard. And all he did was go round to the back of the palace. The harem was at the back.

The nawab's method of selecting a woman from the harem was not, perhaps, untypical among princes, although it is unlikely he used the same method to choose between his European women.

When he entered the harem, he had a stick. The women would pounce on him and pull him and he would keep them back with his stick, until he saw the one he wanted and then he would tell the eunuch.

When Yvonne came to Bahawalpur in 1952 it was soon to be swallowed up by Pakistan. In 1954 the Abbasis lost their right to rule, their hereditary right to decide the life or death of their subjects.

The palace in Bahawalpur, which was slowly being devoured by termites, was a gloomy, secretive place located in the desert where the Punjab meets Sindh. It was said to be the hottest place in India. Yvonne was not much interested in the history of Bahawalpur, and it did not live up to her fantasies of a princely kingdom.

The ancient Rolls Royces still ferried Yvonne and her prince over the potholed roads of Bahawalpur but though they wound the windows up tight, the dust filtered in through every crevice and crack. Begum Yvonne was bored. Bahawalpur was isolated and she had no European company. What use was it to be a princess in a desert where no one saw you being a princess?

Yvonne began to suspect her husband was seeing other women. She had heard about her mother-in-law Linda's death under suspicious circumstances and she began to wonder whether being incarcerated in Bahawalpur's dungeons after his mother's death had affected Riki's sanity. Certainly Bahawalpur was influencing hers. She became increasingly scared and began to suspect plans were afoot to do away with her and keep her sons in Bahawalpur. Certain that she would soon follow in her mother-in-law's footsteps, Yvonne fled the palace for the safety of Sydney.

Recently, Sydney's *Sunday Telegraph* carried various stories supplied by the Public Trustee attempting to track down beneficiaries of unclaimed estates. Among those mentioned was Muriel Martin, who had died in Darlinghurst on 2 July 1994 aged eighty-three. She had been a tireless worker for AIDS charities but no one knew much about her. There was a conspicuous absence of family photos in her Potts Point flat to provide leads as to her relations. The newspaper article did evoke a response, but not from Muriel's daughter Yvonne, whose name the trustee had tracked down through pain-staking research. It was Yvonne's son, Riki Abbasi, who made contact and claimed the $223,000 estate. His mother was incommunicado, he said, and he did not want her upset. He was prepared to put a set of bland questions to his father, Mohamed Abbasi, but Yvonne was not to be disturbed. The nervous breakdowns of which Estelle Stone had spoken had taken their toll.

Yvonne's father-in-law abandoned Bahawalpur after Independence and went to England, taking much of his for-tune with him. He bought a house in Surrey and lived there until his death in 1966. He left behind in Bahawalpur many children, recognized and unrecognized, three palaces, an idle and disorientated harem, some schools and colleges and the ambitious Sutlej Valley Project. The palace in Bahawalpur was eventually sealed and became the subject of litigation.

ANNABELLA PARKER
married Bhagwat Singh, maharana of Udaipur

As a child, Annabella Parker studied ballet at the Royal Ballet School in London with the famous Ninette de Valois, who thought she showed great promise. Her studies came to an end, however, when she was ten and went, with her family, to live in Japan. Her father had been appointed military attaché to the British high commission in Tokyo.

When the Parkers returned to England two years later Annabella knew there was no hope of securing a dancing career. For a while she worked in the foreign office, but she was listless and dissatisfied. She had always pictured herself as a dancer and everything else palled. She dabbled in poetry and longed for some romance in her life – the romance that ballet had given her. In the late 1950's, after she had decided to travel in Asia, she received an invitation from the Chatterji family to visit them in India. Mr Chatterji had been the Indian military attaché in Tokyo while the Parkers had been there and the two families had become close.

Annabella travelled to Bombay where she was met by the Chatterjis. While she was staying with them they suggested she accompany them to Mayo College in Rajasthan, to their son's annual prize-giving. Annabella was delighted at the invitation to travel to Rajasthan and was enchanted – nowhere in India, possibly the world, were beauty, romance and chivalry more revered.

Bhagwat Singh, maharana of Udaipur, one of Mayo's distinguished alumni, was also at the college. At the parents' reception following the prize-giving, Mayo's principal, Jack Gibson, introduced Annabella to the maharana. They were instantly attracted to one another. Bhagwat was struck by Annabella's beauty and she was enchanted by the Rajput romance he embodied. When she told him she would be touring Rajasthan and visiting Delhi and Bombay, Bhagwat offered to drive her to Udaipur, the most romantic of India's cities. She accepted. He subtly romanced her while showing her the sights of Udaipur, then he drove her to Jaipur and left her in the care of the maharajah of Jaipur. He provided her with a sheaf of introductions to India's social elite which enabled her to travel around with ease for the rest of her visit.

Once Annabella was back in Bombay with the Chatterjis, just days before she was due to return to England, a call came through from Bhagwat. He asked her if she would marry him and Annabella accepted. Here was the romance that she had been looking for, combined with wealth and connection.

Bhagwat Singh was born in Udaipur in 1927, the eldest son of a first cousin of the maharana of Udaipur. He showed early promise. The then maharana, Bhupal Singh, had been crippled as a child from polio and was unable to walk unaided. When he failed to produce an heir he adopted Bhagwat Singh, who was in his early teens, although officials put his age as seventeen.

Bhagwat inherited a noble tradition and a long line of fiercely proud ancestors. Fateh Singh, Bhupal's father, was a man of incomparable Rajput honour. Memories of the ferocious battles in which Rajput warriors put on saffron robes and rode to certain death against the Mughals suffused every fibre of his being. Fateh Singh had even taken poison to preserve his honour. When King George V came to India for the Coronation Durbar of 1911 Fateh was expected to attend. But Udaipur only had a gun-salute of nineteen, less than the twenty-one awarded to princes whom Fateh Singh considered to be his inferiors. He could not sit behind rulers whom he looked down upon, nor could he lie and feign illness to the King Emperor. Thus he decided to take just enough poison to make himself genuinely ill so that he would be unable to attend the Durbar. Fateh was also highly suspicious of everyone, except his private secretary, and devised a secret language known only to the two of them, even having coinage inscribed with it.

Bhupal, too, was an eccentric. Every afternoon he drove around Udaipur in an open Rolls Royce, scarlet inside and out, with his aide-de-camp squatting beside him on the floor. Behind travelled three busloads of nobles and servants. Every afternoon he stopped at a general store owned by a Parsi and ordered all the members of his entourage to buy some goods. Bhupal's grandfather had promised the owner's grandfather that if he opened a shop in Udaipur he would give the shop his custom. As a matter of honour, Bhupal felt obliged to follow this tradition.

On Tuesdays, during Bhupal's reign, the British Resident gave a tennis party at his home. Udaipur's nobles and officials would attend, carrying their swords and dressed in their distinctive skirts. On arrival they would drop their swords, tuck up their skirts and take to the court. When Bhupal Singh made an appearance, however, the rackets went down, the skirts went down and the swords went up. Bhupal would give each of the nobles a packet of tobacco to signify they were free for the rest of the day and then watched while they played tennis (swords down, skirts up, rackets up). After twenty minutes, when Bhupal was ready to leave, once again it would be rackets down, skirts down, swords up for his departure.

Maharana Bhagwat Singh and Annabella Parker

When Bhagwat had been officially adopted by Bhupal and had become heir to the throne, a suitable marriage was arranged between him and a Bikaner princess. He was eighteen at the time of the marriage. The couple produced three children: two sons and a daughter. The princess, however, was not a companion with whom Bhagwat could share his many interests. He was a fine sportsman: adept at polo, hockey, cricket, football and tennis. He had completed the Police Training Course at Phillore and passed the Indian Civil Service probationer's examination. A skilled horseman and marksman, he completed an army attachment with the Guides Regiment on the North West Frontier. In business he set up a company and joined with the Taj Group in running the Lake Palace as a luxury hotel.

Annabella let her parents know that she intended to marry Bhagwat, but she did not seek their permission. Looking back, she commented: 'We were both young; it's not something I would recommend people to do. We were lucky our marriage worked out.'

Just weeks after they had met, Annabella and the maharana were married in a civil ceremony at the Bombay Registrar's Office. Though she had access to the famous jewels of Udaipur she wore a simple chiffon tie-dyed sari without jewellery or other ornaments. This was to be her style throughout her married life: understated and elegant.

After the civil ceremony Annabella and Bhagwat drove to Udaipur to have darshan and receive the blessings of the maharana's family deity. The deity resides in the Eklingi Temple, twenty-two kilometres north of Udaipur. Set in a walled complex dating from the eighth century, the temple has a massive pillared hall and a pyramidal roof and is known for its veneration of rats. Annabella found the solemn event a spiritual experience, although she remained a Christian.

In addition to the fairytale City Palace in Udaipur, which is the largest palace complex in Rajasthan and stands on the shores of Lake Pichola, Bhagwat owned a variety of other palaces and homes, most notably the Lake Palace and the Jagmandir Palace which are built on islands in Lake Pichola. He also owned the Shikarbadi hunting lodge, about three kilometres out of town, which was once the royal hunting lodge, and a house in Mount Abu, Rajasthan's only hill station. He had a flat each in Bombay and in London's Abbey Road.

Annabella and Bhagwat lived in the City Palace when they were in Udaipur. A journalist describes it:

> The heart of the palace proper was a grandiloquent dream landscape of domes and turrets, balconies and gardens: there were miles of marble corridors and great courtyards whose walls were covered with brightly painted scenes from the campaigns of Pratap Singh. Light rainbowed into the royal bedchambers through fretworked windows filled with coloured glass. On the upper stories were hanging gardens with splashing fountains, blankets of flowers, and marble paths leading beneath pomegranate and orange trees. Clouds of green parrots billowed and spun above the gardens in the evenings, and peacocks preened and shimmered in the battlements.

Annabella had her own rooms with marble jalis (windows of carved stone) and mirror mosaic ceilings. Despite their beauty, however, her rooms were a little shabby, and there was always trouble with the plumbing in the mosaic and marble bathrooms. She knew that the maharana's first wife, who was living in strict purdah, did not approve of the marriage. When Annabella came to Udaipur, Bhagwat's first wife was not living

Annabella Parker, maharani of Udaipur

in the palace, but she later came back and lived in her own apartments. She and Annabella were never to meet. Annabella doubted that Bhagwat would have married her if he had not already married according to tradition and produced a son and heir.

In accordance with custom, Annabella always wore a sari, favouring soft flowing chiffons. She tried to learn Hindi from a pandit appointed by Bhagwat but she found the servants' inabilty to understand her faltering Hindi discouraging. She was left alone in the palace a good deal and seldom saw Bhagwat during the day as he was busy seeing to the family's financial ventures and fulfilling commitments involved with being the director of numerous charitable and religious trusts. The family was usually together for drinks and dinner in the evenings. Indian food did not agree with Annabella, so her food was prepared separately and this proved a wedge between her and Bhagwat and his family.

A combination of being a foreigner, being the maharana's second wife and being married to the ruler of India's most ancient and orthodox kingdom, limited Annabella's acceptance and resulted in her having little influence in the household. She sensed that Bhagwat's two sons resented her. Their mother, Bhagwat's first wife, had a coterie of friends and palace retainers and when Bhagwat was away power inevitably lay with her sons.

To while away the hours, Annabella occupied herself composing poetry, typing correspondence associated with her position as the director for India of the Royal Society for the Protection of Animals and travelling around rescuing dogs and other maltreated animals. From the time she arrived in India, she had been concerned at the plight of many of the animals she saw, and had been impressed when Bhagwat had told her that in Udaipur it was a criminal offence to kill a monkey or a peacock. Bhagwat supported her animal welfare work as long as she did not use her title 'maharani'.

She met many people through this work. Foreigners and Parsis were not concerned about her association with sick animals, although Hindus considered working with animals unseemly for a woman.

One of the poems Annabella wrote was 'Evening on Jagmandir', which is about the view at dusk from the City Palace. The following extract gives an idea of the beauty of the scene that must have inspired her:

> A ripple as the lake is stirred,
> The scent of flowers is strong and clear,
> sleepy twitter still is heard,
> And night has come to Jagmandir.
>
> The beauty of the evening light,
> The enchantment of the land,
> The loaming shimmer of marble white,
> The chatter of a parrot band.
> If all this beauty here doth make
> A man create a dream.
> I wish, O Rana of the Lake,
> That we may now redeem
> The honour that which once was ours,
> The noble thoughts, the brave new deeds,
> The self-respect, the love of God,
> The feeling for each other's needs.

Despite its beauty, Udaipur proved stifling for Annabella. While being a premier state among the Rajput kingdoms, it had always prided itself on its heroic warrior and conservative traditions. Though Annabella and Bhagwat accompanied

Annabella Parker at home in the City Palace, Udaipur

overseas visitors on sight-seeing tours of India, during their eighteen years together they never officially visited other princely states as a couple. Nor did Annabella ever attend any princely weddings with her husband because, as she explained, 'she was a foreigner'. In orthodox Rajput states purdah was as strictly observed as it was in the Muslim courts. Annabella therefore never accompanied her husband to festivities because 'only men attended'. She was permitted, however, as royal women for generations had been, to watch what went on on festival days from the pierced stone windows of the palace.

Bombay permitted more freedom than Udaipur, and Annabella and Bhagwat would spend every other month in their Bombay apartment. Here Annabella could go shopping and do all the things a Western wife would normally do. In Bombay the Singhs had numerous friends, many of them

Annabella had to pursue her interest in Indian dance in private

westernized and sophisticated Parsis who were unconcerned about Annabella being English. Here Annabella was able to pursue her interest in Indian dance and with Bhagwat's agreement she hired a teacher to instruct her privately. Bhagwat would never agree to watch her perform, however, as he nursed the traditional prejudice against dancers that had arisen from their past association with prostitution. Because she was required by Bhagwat to keep her dancing lessons a secret, and was never given the opportunity to perform in front of anyone, Annabella eventually lost interest in this complex and beautiful art form.

Eighteen years of married life spent in India passed quickly. However, Annabella was suddenly recalled to England to nurse her mother, who had suffered a severe stroke. When her mother died Annabella's elderly, frail father was devastated and depended on Annabella to make the funeral arrangements and to provide him with support.

Back in Udaipur Bhagwat and his eldest son, Mahendra Singh, were fighting over custody of family property. Mentally troubled and ill, Bhagwat was devastated that his son had turned on him. The dispute resulted in Bhagwat's health declining further, and while she was still in England with her father Annabella received a phone call announcing that he had died of a heart attack. She was advised not to return immediately – being a woman she would be unable to attend his funeral. She settled her father as best she could, promised to return as soon as possible, and left for Udaipur.

Annabella knew what was expected of an Indian widow. She would have to wear white for a year and would be unable to attend any social functions. She would also be expected to conduct herself quietly. These restrictions were not difficult for her, for by nature she was serious and modest. She was careful to appear in public well groomed, however, and, as usual, she wore lipstick. This offended her husband's eldest son. She felt unwelcome and so returned to her father in England, leaving her belongings in her apartment in the palace.

Bhagwat's eldest son, Mahendra, became maharana of Udaipur, but Bhagwat had made sure that most of the property went to the younger brother, Arvind Singh. In 1984, after getting drunk at a party, the new maharana took a group of supporters to the City Palace and tried to force his way inside. The police came and locked the palace, refusing anyone entry until the property dispute was sorted out. The palace was finally reopened in 1988, at which time Annabella could have collected her possessions, but she had no wish to return to Udaipur.

Today, Annabella has remarried and she and her husband live in England, in the New Forest. She continues to be director for India of the Royal Society for the Protection of Animals.

HELEN SIMMONS

married Mukarram Jah Bahadur, nizam of Hyderabad

*A*ustralian Helen Simmons was of Irish-Scots ancestry and lived in Perth. She was one of three sisters in a close family. In 1971, at the age of twenty-one, she left home to 'do Europe', as many young women of her generation did. After working at various jobs, including one at the drama department of the BBC and being a nanny, she returned to Perth and became secretary to millionaire architect Yosse Goldberg. With her warm, outgoing personality, Helen soon became Yosse's friend and was often a guest at his dinner parties. It was at Yosse's house that she met Mukarram Jah.

Mukarram Jah was born in Paris in 1933. He was educated at Doon School, then Harrow, in England. He went to Cambridge University where he read history, and then went on to Sandhurst Military College. In 1960, in London, he married Esra Birgin, a Turkish language student. They were living in London when, seven years later, he heard that his grandfather, Sir Osman Ali Khan, the seventh nizam of Hyderabad, had died and had chosen Jah as his successor. Jah came into a fortune estimated at $2,000 million.

In 1972, disillusioned with life in India, Jah came to Perth and settled on a vast sheep station called Murchison, west of Kalbarri, 650 miles from Perth. Esra did not take to life in rural Australia and after ten days left for Hyderabad and London. Jah had been alone for four years by the time he met Helen.

Hyderabad was the largest of all the princely states – larger than England and Scotland combined – and one of the richest. Much of the nizams' legendary wealth was drawn from the mines of Golconda which had, since their opening, disgorged 12,000,000 carats of diamonds into the world market. In addition to the diamond mines were the Kolar goldfields which were worked intensively under the nizams to produce a steady stream of gold until the pickings became too meagre to justify their running.

The sixth nizam, Sir Mahbub Ali Khan, born in 1866, was said to have kept the most exotic and lavish court in India. He was an excellent polo player, a crack shot and a generous host. His court was a cultured domain employing the finest musicians, singers and painters from throughout India. His prime minister, Sir Salar Jung, gathered together oustanding artworks from around the world and lodged them in a repository that is now the Salar Jung Museum. The British approved of Sir Salar Jung because of his administrative ability and for his efforts at keeping a check upon the outrageous extravagances of his master. He was greatly mourned when he died suddenly after dining too well at a picnic on canned oysters.

Sir Mahbub was eccentric, reclusive and solitary. Much of his 'queerness' the British attributed to the fact that he had spent his early life dominated by the women of the harem.

Sir Mahbub's family were noted for their unconventionality. His sister kept an armed guard of amazonian women to look after her in her declining years, and his son, the seventh nizam, Sir Osman Ali Khan, had unusual interests. He was a passionate adherent of unani medicine, an ancient Greek system, the basis of which was the action of powdered jewels administered in infusions of herbs or in syrups. Sir Osman employed unani remedies for many of his physical ills. He was also interested in photography. After his death a cache of bizarre photographs were found that had been taken with a hidden camera inside his guest bathroom. They provide a candid record of his famous visitors performing their toilet.

Like his ancestors before him, Sir Osman spent much of his time within the harem and his paternal exploits were legendary. It is said that he sired a total of two hundred children.

In 1945 Hyderabad was said to have had $250,000 in gold bullion and two billion dollars in coin and precious stones. Sir Osman Ali Khan's collection of jewels was reputedly the largest in the world. His collections of Grecian silver, jade and crystal were exquisite. He also collected spectacles and rolls of banknotes which in time were gnawed into confetti by rats.

In 1995, Sir Osman's heirs were finally given permission by the Indian government to sell his 173-item jewel collection. Forty per cent of the money from the sales went to Mukarram Jah. Wrote *India Today*,

> When the contents of the three steel trunks were emptied onto the table in the airless Hongkong Bank room in south Bombay last fortnight, a hush descended on the people crowded around. The unspeakable lustre and exquisite craftsmanship of the Asaf Jahi rubies, emeralds and diamonds commanded awe and admiration. As the item-by-item inspection began, Jayant N. Chawlera, the Government's valuer, picked up the sparkling Jacob Diamond and touched his forehead with it reverentially.

The collection was said to 'have came from the Mughals' scattered treasuries, the kingdoms of Vijayanagar, Bidar and Golconda and from the czars of Russia. So exquisite was it

that the auction attracted sultans, shipping tycoons and
financiers, including the sultan of Brunei, Greek shipowner
Stavros Niarchos and Dubai banker Abdul Wahab Galadhari.

The Jacob diamond, the centrepiece of the nizam's jewels,
is the world's third best in whiteness and seventh in size. *India
Today* wrote of the diamond,

> Believed to have been mined in Africa and bought
> in London by a Shimla-based Jewish trader, A.M.
> Jacob – after whom it is named – the gem was sold
> by him to the sixth Nizam Mahbub Ali Khan in the
> nineteenth century.

Alexander Jacob was a fascinating character and was known
for his magical powers. He was the most important dealer of
jewels and antiquities in India and worked as a spy for the
Government of India. In spite of his many abilities, however,
he was outwitted by the nizam, who paid him only half the
price of the Jacob diamond, despite considerable litigation.
The legal expenses beggared Jacob, who died a broken man.
The case brought opprobrium upon the nizam who, in shame
and disgust, wrapped the diamond in a cloth and dropped it
in a drawer. Eventually it was discovered by the seventh nizam
in the toe of one of his father's slippers. He had a gold filigree
base made for it and thereafter used it as a paperweight.

It was into this remarkable family that Helen married. After
their meeting at Yosse Goldberg's, the couple had soon fallen
in love. Helen thought Jah was handsome, and was captivated
by his 'bottomless brown eyes' and his gentle nature. Jah was
taken by Helen's freshness, good humour and lack of snobbishness. They spent much of their time together at his vast
sheep station, Murchison House, and there were picnics at his
beach house. She became a Muslim, taking the name Aysha,

and she and Jah were married in 1979 in a Muslim ceremony when she was eight months pregnant with her first son, Alexander Azam.

Azam's birth prompted Esra, Jah's first wife, to take action to secure the inheritance of her two children and she came to Perth that year for the divorce proceedings.

In 1981, Helen and Jah were married in a civil ceremony and Helen, aged thirty-one, became the Begum of Hyderabad. In 1983 she gave birth to a second son, Umar. In the early years of their marriage, bowing to Jah's obsession with privacy, Helen was happy to simply spend her days with him and their two boys. Their social life consisted of select dinner parties, taking in a movie or dinner at a restaurant.

In 1984 Jah took Helen on a visit to Europe and then to India. Helen found Hyderabad stifling and Mukarram's palaces seedy and decrepit. She talked to friends of visiting crumbling palaces suffocated in jungle, crystal and chandeliers the size of single-bedroom apartments lying broken and colonized by pigeons. She had not realized the restrictions that would be placed upon her as a Muslim wife and found it difficult to contend with the army of sycophants who surrounded her husband. She was appalled at the way his family and staff were appropriating his property. In addition the income tax department and Central Bureau of Intelligence were breathing down his neck.

Helen and Mukarram Jah stayed at the Chiran Palace high in the Banjara Hills which covered an area of 395 acres. But it was modest in size compared with his other Hyderabadi palaces: the King Kothi Palace, Parade Villa, and the Falaknuma. The Falaknuma, built of Italian marble and considered by some to be the most magnificent palace in India, had a priceless collection of paintings, statues and English furniture and was used in the seventh nizam's time as a royal guest house.

Today it is leased by the Taj Hotel Group, which runs it as a five-star hotel.

There was also the hundred-acre Naukhanda Palace, the Himayat Bagh Palace and the ninety-four-acre Ahmed Bagh Palace. And finally, the most beautiful palace, the Chowmahalla, where state receptions and durbars were held.

> The main quadrangle has a beautiful garden surrounding a large marble cistern, the fountains and splashing waters which in moonlit nights can be compared to the enchanted garden described in the Arabian Nights.

Jah was unable to share his financial worries with Helen for even he was unable to grasp the scale of deceit wrought by his so-called advisers. Jah's lawyer, R. Balasubramanian, had complained about him to the Hyderabad police, but they well knew that it was the managers of Jah's properties that had plundered the valuable artefacts, the paintings, the porcelain and antiques. Local toughs took over some of the Chowmahalla Palace grounds while a retainer usurped an eighteen-acre farm near Hyderabad. As Jah's former secretary explained: 'Sycophants and fly-by-night operators have landed him in this mess.'

Helen was appalled to learn that the Chiran Palace was at risk of being appropriated. Jah's staff had signed an agreement to sell about 250 acres of the palace to a cooperative housing society. Parade Villa in Hyderabad, a property in Aurangabad, the Naukhanda Palace and the Himayat Bagh Palace – all were being variously plundered.

After several months, Helen had had enough and gave Jah an ultimatum. He agreed to return with her to Australia and did not return to Hyderabad and attempt to sort out his affairs until after her death.

Jah needed little urging to return to Western Australia. He preferred living at Murchison House Station, away from the social glare which he abhorred. In time, however, Helen began to chafe against the quietness of her life and began putting out feelers to Perth society. She chose to spend increasing amounts of time at their historic Perth mansion, Havelock House, which Jah had bought in 1979.

One of the first major social events she attended was a charity function held in 1983 at the home of Perth millionaire Kerry Stokes. It was here she met a cousin of Kerry Stokes', Peter Forbes, and they soon became close friends. Peter had no money of his own and survived by making himself useful and amusing to rich patrons. He was an inveterate party-goer and he quickly drew Helen into the limelight. At Helen's insistence Forbes was hired by Jah to drive Helen to appointments, organize her dinner parties and shop for groceries. He became her 'walker', escorting her to Perth's elite parties and exclusive nightclubs.

Helen bought a Triumph Stag sportscar, and could be seen whipping around Perth with Peter at her side. Jah had difficulty accepting the freer side of Helen's life and the fact that she had platonic men friends.

Helen's debut into Perth society came at a fashion parade held by Perth's upmarket boutique Elle in 1985. Her impact was described by the fashion magazine, *Follow Me*:

> She took a tableful of friends that night, arrived fashionably late and featured a blinding array of the fabled Indian jewels. If the smart set had been itching to find out who this princess was, they got an eyeful that night.

From that night on Helen was seldom out of the limelight, and wherever Helen went, Peter went too, despite the fact that Helen must have been aware that he was known for 'sponging off wealthy women'. One of the city's newspaper editors described Forbes as someone 'who had a big heart to give unhappy wealthy women and they loved him for it'.

As time passed, Helen found that constantly being in the social columns had its downside. Each time her name appeared in the newspapers

> ... the phone calls and letters she'd get – people asking for things, saying how disgusting it was her wearing all that jewellery, having all that money. It was just another pressure.

By early 1986, Helen was becoming disillusioned with her life. She and her husband were no longer close. Many of her so-called friends were taking advantage of her wealth and were using her pulling power to sell tickets to society soirees. She had a nervous breakdown and suffered migraines. People were making fun of her growing obesity.

It was at this time that she held a large charity cocktail party at Havelock House and met Peter Forbes's new lover. Jah was absent, as he always was on social occasions, and the young man lavished attention on her. Charming, witty and sophisticated, he was also a great dancer, and Helen was enchanted. Peter was appalled at what was going on but was powerless to stop it.

Within six weeks Helen had established the young man in a townhouse in a beachside suburb. She tried to keep the relationship secret but it was not long before Forbes, bitter about his betrayal by his lover and Helen, spread the story around town. People began to take sides, most of them siding with Forbes who had been so publicly humiliated.

Helen Simmons

Later in the year she began getting recurrent sore throats and swollen glands. In February 1987 she was found to be HIV-positive, as was her young man. She was shattered by the news but it also steeled her to live what life she had on her own terms. She asked Jah for a divorce, to which he reluctantly agreed, and is reputed to have received a settlement of half a billion dollars.

Helen moved into a rented house, while one she had bought was being renovated, and continued to see her young lover. She withdrew from society and saw few friends. Her illness made her feel unclean and she was bitter and angry. Her sister Julie said later,

> We all believe Helen died long before she actually did. She just wasn't the Helen we knew at all. And when Peter Forbes died, she went downhill rapidly. In a bizarre sort of way she blamed Peter. No doubt about it. She didn't think of her young man. If you love someone, you follow your feelings.

Peter Forbes was diagnosed as HIV-positive in June 1987. He let it be known he had contracted the virus from his and Helen's lover and spread the news of Helen's condition. It spread like wildfire throughout Perth society. He had a huge fortieth birthday party a few months later, popping his AZT tablets between cocktails, and died in February 1988, never having forgiven Helen.

Helen died in Royal Perth Hospital in early May 1989. Her parents, who only found out about her condition when she was admitted to hospital, were with her, as was Jah. Interviewed by the *Sydney Morning Herald* a year later, Jah said that he had not yet come to terms with her death. 'I used to visit her nearly every afternoon ... and we would have long talks together. It was agonizing to see her gradually dying.'

At first the media reported 'Partygoer princess dies at 41 after a long illness', but then the story came out and Helen's reputation, according to Julie, was dragged 'well and truly through the mud'. The media reported that Perth society was AIDS-ridden and that Helen had spread it.

The public response was hysterical. Journalist Steve McLeod responded, in *Follow Me* magazine,

> Helen's tragic death, born of a lonely woman's desperate attempt for passion and happiness, brought bubbling to the surface the shameless accusers and fear-peddlers who exploit scandal. It also caused questions to be asked in kinder circles about what kind of compassion our society is capable of. Will it take a similarly public tragedy for the same questions to be asked in the rest of the country? Or will Princess Helen's death be the last headlined, head-hunted media AIDS horror story?

Helen's sister Rhonda took Jah and Helen's sons into her care when Helen became ill, and following her death Jah entrusted the boys to her care, as Helen had requested. Helen felt that Jah was too much of a nomad to be able to look after his sons properly, but he sees them regularly.

To scotch rumours among his people and to allay his own fears, Jah had blood tests done in Switzerland that proved negative. Only a few months after Helen's death, he let it be known he was in the market for a new wife.

In Istanbul he was introduced to several women but none, he says, impressed as 'the sort of girl who would open a station gate'. One night, at a party at a kebab house on the Bosphorous, he met Manolya Onur, a former Miss Turkey. He and Manolya married in August 1990 and had a daughter. Officially the marriage foundered on arguments about domicile, with Manolya wanting to live in Istanbul and Jah insisting that they live in Perth. His palace retainers tell a different story, however, claiming that the marriage fell apart when Onur found out about his Moroccan mistress Jameela Boularous.

Several more marriages followed. It was as though Jah was heeding the call of cultural memory, following in the footsteps of his ancestors for whom a string of wives and concubines was not exceptional. And it was the stirrings of that old culture that destroyed his and Helen's happiness.

REFERENCES

Archives

United Kingdom
India Office Library and Records, London
National Film Archive, London
Reuters Television Archive, London
Royal Archives, Windsor Castle
P.&O. Company Archives, London
National Maritime Museum, Greenwich
Probate Office, London

Australia
Australian Archives, Canberra
Government House Archives, Sydney
University of Melbourne Archives, Parkville
Supreme Court of New South Wales
Supreme Court of Victoria, Probates Division
The Public Trustee, Victoria
Archives of the Victorian Health Commission

United States of America
Federal Bureau of Investigation, Washington

France
Registres de l'etat civil, Cannes
Registres de l'etat civil, Neuilly

India
Tamil Nadu Archives, Chennai
National Archives of India, Delhi

Newspapers and Periodicals

Advertiser (Adelaide)
Amrita Bazar Patrika (Kolkata)
Blue Mountains Advertiser (Katoomba)
Blue Mountains Echo (Katoomba)
Bombay Chronicle
Bulletin (Sydney)
Bystander (London)
Civil and Military Gazette
Daily Mail
Honolulu Star Bulletin
Illustrated London News
India Magazine
India Today
International Herald Tribune
Melbourne Punch
New York Star Sun
New York Times
New York World Telegram
Pastoral Review
Post and Rail
Princely India
Sunday Graphic (London)
Sketch
Star (London)
Sydney Morning Herald
Tatler
Walkabout
West Australian

Unpublished Sources

Correspondence with Elsie Kunz, Yuvraj Digvijay Sinh of Wankaner, Nawab Iqbal Khan of Palanpur, Jamsaheb of Jamnagar, Maharajah Gaj Singh of Jodhpur, Professor Sandy Yarwood and Sister Eugenie (author's private collection)
Letters from Rajah Martanda Bhairava Tondaiman (Professor Smyth collection)

Elsie Thompson and Maharajah Tikari, Myrtle McLeod, High Commission of India and S.L. Polak (Kunz family collection)

Thompson Family History (Kunz family collection)

Audio tapes of Maharani Annabella of Udaipur (author's collection)

16 mm footage of Joan Palanpur (Yuvraj Digvijay Sinh of Wankaner collection)

Video footage of John Wakefield, Bob Wright, Princess Beryl of Jind, Prince Singh of Tumkohi, Ruskin Bond, Maharani Prithvibir of Jind and Yuvraj Digvijay Sinh (author's collection)

Books

Abdullah, Morag, Murray, *My Khyber Marriage: Experiences of a Scotswoman as the wife of a Pathan Chieftan's Son*, London: George C. Harrap, 1934.

Aiyar, S.R., *General History of Pudukkottai State*, Pudukkottai: Sri Brihadamba Press, 1916.

Alexander, Michael and Anand, Sushila, *Queen Victoria's Maharajah Duleep Singh 1838–93*, London: Weidenfeld and Nicolson, 1988.

Allen, C. (ed.) *Plain Tales from the Raj: Images of British India in the Twentieth Century*, London: Andre Deutsch, 1975.

—— *Raj: A Scrapbook of British India 1877–1947*, London: Andre Deutsch, 1977.

Allen Charles and Dwivedi, Sharada, *Lives of the Indian Princes*, London: Century, 1984.

Anderson, Carol (ed.), *Violet Jacob Diaries and Letters from India 1895–1900*, Edinburgh: Canongate, 1990.

Ballhatchet, K., *Race, Sex and Class under the Raj*, London: Weidenfeld and Nicolson, 1980.

Barr, Pat, *The Memsahibs: The Women of Victorian India*, London: Secker and Warburg, 1976.

—— *The Dust in the Balance: British Women in India 1905–1945*, London: Hamish Hamilton, 1989.

Barr, Pat and Desmond, Ray, *Simla: A Hill Station in British India*, London: The Scholar Press, 1978.

Bence-Jones, Mark, *The Viceroys of India*, London: Constable, 1982.

Birkett, Dea, *Spinsters Abroad: Victorian Lady Explorers*, Oxford: Basil Blackwell, 1989.

Bond, Ruskin and Saili, Ganesh, *Mussoorie and Landour*, New Delhi: Lustre Press, 1992.

Bolt, C., *Victorian Attitudes to Race*, London: Routledge and Kegan Paul, 1971.

Brinda, Maharani of Kapurthala, *Maharani: The Story of an Indian Princess*, New York: Henry Holt, 1954.

Campbell, Christy, *The Maharajah's Box*, London: HarperCollins, 2000.

Chew, Shirley and Rutherford, Anna, *Unbecoming Daughters of the Empire*, Sydney: Dangaroo Press, 1993.

Chudgar, P.L., *Indian Princes Under British Protection*, London: Williams and Norgate, 1929.

Cooch Behar, Maharani of, *The Autobiography of an Indian Princess*, London: John Murray, 1921.

Copland, Ian, *The Princes of India in the Endgame of Empire, 1917–1947*, Cambridge: Cambridge University Press, 1997.

Corfield, Sir Conrad, *The Princely India I knew from Reading to Mountbatten*, Madras: George Thomas, 1975.

Crossette, Barbara, *The Great Hill Stations of Asia*, Colorado: Westview Press, 1998.

Curzon, Marquess of Keddleston, *Leaves from a Viceroy's Note-Book and Other Papers*, London: Macmillan, 1926.

Dass, Diwan Jarmani and Dass, Rakesh Bhan, *Maharani*, New Delhi: Orient, 1972.

Devi, Gayatri and Rama Rau, Santha, *The Memoirs of the Maharani of Jaipur*, Philadelphia: Lipincott, 1976.

Diver, Maud, *Royal India*, London: Hodder and Stoughton, 1942.

Douds, G.J., *Government and Princes: India 1918–1939*, Ph.D. thesis, University of Edinburgh, 1979.

Devi, Gayatri and Rama Rau, S., *A Princess Remembers: The Memoirs of the Maharani of Jaipur*, London: Weidenfeld and Nicolson, 1976.

Duyker, Edward and Younger, Coralie, *Molly and the Rajah: Race, Romance and the Raj*, Sydney: Australian Mauritian Press, 1991.

Evans, Hubert, *Looking Back on India*, London: Frank Cass, 1988.

Falkiner, Suzanne, *Haddon Rig: The First Hundred Years*, Woollahra: Valadon Press, 1981.

Fitze, Sir Kenneth, *Twilight of the Maharajahs*, London: John Murray, 1956.

Fitzroy, Yvonne, *Courts and Camps in India*, London: Methuen, 1926.

Forbes, Rosita, *India of the Princes*, London: The Book Club, 1939.

Fraser, Sir Andrew, *Among Indian Rajahs and Ryots*, London: Seeley, Service and Co., 1912.

French, Patrick, Younghusband, *The Last Great Imperial Adventurer*, London: HarperCollins, 1994.

Galbraith, J.K., *Ambassador's Journal*, London: Hamish Hamilton, 1969.

Graves, C., *Royal Riviera*, London: Heinemann, 1957.

Henderson, A., *Henderson's Australian Families*, Melbourne: A. Henderson, 1941.

Irvine, Lt. Col. A.A., *Land of No Regrets*, London: Collins, 1938.

Jeffrey, Robin (ed.), *People, Princes and Paramount Power: Society and Politics in the Indian Princely States*, Delhi: Oxford University Press, 1978.

Jhabvala, Ruth Prawer, *Heat and Dust*, London: John Murray, 1975.

Joardar, B., *Prostitution in Nineteenth and Early Twentieth Century Calcutta*, New Delhi: Inter-India Publications, 1985.

Kanwar, Pamela, *Imperial Simla: The Political Culture of the Raj*, Delhi: Oxford University Press, 1990.

Kennedy, Dane, *The Magic Mountains Hill Stations and the British Raj*, Berkeley: University of California Press, 1996.

Kincaid, Dennis, *British Social Life in India 1608–1937*, Delhi: Routledge and Kegan Paul, 1973.

King, Anthony, *Colonial Urban Development: Culture, Social Power and Environment*, London: Routledge and Kegan Paul, 1984.

Kulkarni, V.B., *Princely India and Lapse of British Paramountcy*, Bombay: Jaico, 1985.

Lord, John, *The Maharajahs*, London: Hutchinson and Co., 1972.

Lancaster, O., *With an Eye to the Future*, London: John Murray, 1967.

McMillan, Margaret, *Women of the Raj*, London: Thames and Hudson, 1988.

Menon, K.P.S., *Many Worlds*, London: Oxford University Press, 1965.

Moorhouse, Geoffrey, *Om: An Indian Pilgrimage*, London: Sceptre, 1994.

Morrow, Ann, *Highness*, London:

Muthiah, S., *The Spencer Legend*, Chennai: Eastwest Books, 1997.

Natwar Singh, K., *The Magnificent Maharajah: The Life and Times of Maharaja Bhupinder Singh of Patiala 1891–1938*, New Delhi: HarperCollins, 1998.

Palmer, Alan, *The East End: Four Centuries of London Life*, London: John Murray, 1989.

Panter-Downes, Mollie, *Ooty Preserved: A Victorian Hill Station*, London: Hamish Hamilton, 1967.

Plumptre, G., *The Fast Set: The World of Edwardian Racing*, London: Andre Deutsch, 1985.

Ramsack, B.N., *The Princes of India in the Twilight of Empire*, Columbus: Ohio State University Press, 1978.

Robins, Leslie, *Policing the Raj*, London: The Chamelon Press, 1985.

Rose, K., *King George V*, New York: Alfred A. Knopf, 1984.

Rutledge, Helen (ed.), *A Season In India: Letters of Ruby Madden – Experiences of an Australian Girl at The Great Coronation Durbar Delhi: 1903*, South Australia: Fontana/Collins, 1976.

Seaver, George, *Francis Younghusband*, London: John Murray, 1952.

Sorabji, Cornelia, *India Calling: The Memories of Cornelia Sorabji*, London: Nisbet and Co., 1934.

Spear, Percival, *The Oxford History of Modern India 1745–1975*, Delhi: Oxford University Press, 1978.

Thompson, E., *The Making of the Indian Princes*, London: Oxford University Press, 1943.

Tottenham, E.L., *Highnesses of Hindostan*, London: Grayson and Grayson, 1934.

Trevelyan, H., *The India We Left*, London: Macmillan, 1972.

Vansittart, Jane, *From Minnie with Love*, London: Peter Davies, 1974.

Vazquez de Gey, Elisa, *Anita Delgado: Maharani de Kapurthala*, Barcelona: O Planeta, 1998.

West, John, *Theatre in Australia*, Sydney: Cassell and Co., 1978.

Westlake, Graeme D., *An Introduction to the Hill Stations of India*, New Delhi: Indus Publishing, 1993.

Wild, Roland, *Ranjitsinhji*, London: Rich and Cowan Limited, 1934.

Wolpert, Stanley, *India*, Berkeley: University of California Press, 1991.

Worswick, Clark, *Princely India: Photographs by Raja Deen Dayal 1884–1910*, New York: Pennwick, 1980.

Younger, Coralie, *Anglo-Indians: Neglected Children of the Raj*, New Delhi: B.R. Publishing, 1987.

Yule, H. and Burnett, A.C., *Hobson-Jobson* (first published 1886), London: Routledge and Kegan Paul, 1969.